Growing a
Mother's Heart

Growing a
Mother's Heart

❈ ❈ ❈

Bible Study

Be loving!
Karen Whiting
1 John 4:7

Karen Whiting

AMG
PUBLISHERS

Growing a Mother's Heart
Bible Study

Copyright © 2022 by Karen Whiting

Published by AMG Publishers
6815 Shallowford Road
Chattanooga, Tennessee 37421

ISBN 13: 978-1-61715-569-7 Paper Back

First Printing—April 2022

Cover designed by Brian Wooten, Brikwoo Creative Group, Chattanooga, Tennessee
Editing by BookBaby Publishing Interior design, and typesetting by Perfec-Type, Nashville, Tennessee

Printed in the United States of America

Dedication

Dedicated in Memory of
My Mother and Grandmothers

Marie Hartigan

Grandma Nora Doody

Grandma Marion Hartigan

Great Grandma Edith Read

TABLE OF CONTENTS

Note: In *Growing a Mother's Heart* some names were changed. The Bible Study uses all the actual names.

WELCOME!

This study is a companion book to book *Growing a Mother's Heart: Devotions of Faith, Hope, and Love, From Mothers Past, Present, and Future.*

Made for busy moms, the lessons are not long and include practical tips and ideas to apply in a mother's life. The book contains scriptures, prayers and devotional stories that show how various principles and ideas work in action. In week one we consider the times when we feel inadequate and know we missed the mark, such as times we messed up or a child wandered off in seconds. Those relate to similar (sometimes the same) stories in the book *Growing a Mother's Heart*. We share bonds as moms with stories of our real lives. We learn through those stories and from one another.

With God's blessings, we continue to grow our mom's hearts. God chose us to be mothers and with God's help, we'll be good enough.

We also learn from studying scriptures and discovering God's wisdom. We'll look beyond the stories to find solutions and the comfort and guidance of God's Word.

Applications let us understand Biblical principles and weave in ideas to help in daily life. For example, as we read about tiredness, we also explore scriptures related to various types of rest needed. In exploring hospitality and meals, we'll read about various meals in the Bible and the reasons for those meals. Studies show the importance of meals for families, so the tips in the study provide tips to make mealtime go smoother.

Hopefully, you will enjoy this study in a group with the fellowship of other moms. You'll add your stories, share tips of what works for you, and discuss the scriptures and how they help integrate faith in your family life.

May you be blessed as you study and share with your friends!

WEEK 1

Breathless Days and Endless Nights

Weeks in *Growing a Mother's Heart* that coordinate with this week's study

Week 15: Perchance to Sleep

Week 18: How Can I Calm My Anxious Heart?

Week 21: Around the Table

DAY 1

Blessed as Moms
Amid the Chaos

"You're blessed when you're at the end of your rope.
With less of you there is more of God and his rule.
"You're blessed when you feel you've lost what is
most dear to you. Only then can you be embraced
by the One most dear to you." MATTHEW 5:3-4 MSG

"Mom!" My four-year-old Becky strutted in, hands on hips.
"I told Michael not to do it, but he did it anyway, and made a
gigantic mess. I tried to clean it up, but he made it worse."

I panicked, with only ten minutes left to be ready. This
first outing with our third child seemed challenging. At
age four, Becky prided herself on being my little helper.
Michael, at twenty months, enjoyed fun and bounced
everywhere. He never saw the messes he created. James
at three weeks lay quietly in his crib. My husband's ship-
mates (he served on a Coast Guard cutter) had planned a
luncheon for us to celebrate the birth of James. The cap-
tain's wife (experienced mom of four) offered to pick us up
(car seats to be switched and all).

Alas, Michael had dumped shampoo all over the floor. Becky had tried to clean it up by sprinkling on baby powder (she said it dried a bottom so why not a floor) while Michael bounced under her to feel the falling snow. My white dappled son laughed and slid on the floor, with powder sprinkled all over him and his clothes. Becky had remained clean, so I sent her to watch the baby and thus keep her out of trouble. I suppressed giggles when Michael grinned at me. I closed the bathroom door, hoping that, when I returned home, it would not be a solidified, sticky mess. I washed him, changed his clothes, and kept myself clean by tucking an old towel under my chin.

The doorbell rang and my daughter's voice soon related every detail of our morning. Horrified, I dashed out to greet Judy. She had already grabbed a mop and was cleaning the floor. She grinned and suggested I remove my large towel bib before we left.

––––––––––––

We all have days when plans don't turn out picture perfect and things take an unexpected twist. Thankfully, later (sometimes much later) we look back and laugh at those moments. Motherhood is messy, hard work, and yet a great blessing.

Sometimes we stress out.

> *Sometimes* the giggles and sweet attempts of help from our precious children keep us sane.

>> *Sometimes* God sends an angel to our rescue.

Consider a day that seemed to go wrong from the start or when you felt like you were at the end of your rope and wanted to turn in your mom badge.

What happened? _Tried taking them to costco and chick fil-a. They lost it, Haddie screamed all day. Jojo kept hurting everyone._

How did you react? _I gripped her arm too tight._

_____

_____

What melted your heart and helped you smile again?

At the end of the night all three played nicely and let me clean up from dinner.

_____

The Beatitudes

Jesus surprised listeners when He preached something from a different perspective than what people usually thought. Blessed is the translation of the Greek word *makarios*. It means happy or spiritually prosperous. Each one reveals values the opposite of what the world believes. Jesus urged people to think from an eternal perspective.

Being stressed from motherhood makes a woman weary, but it also brings great blessings. God beckons us to find blessings when we feel challenged.

List blessings of having children even when you're tired and stressed:

Their giggles, hugs, and stories.

Songs.

How does motherhood cause you to depend more on God and less on your own abilities?

I fail everytime and I'll keep failing. Only He can

give me the strength and patience to do this.

Read Matthew 5:1-12. The Beatitudes challenge our attitudes and priorities because Jesus gives each characteristic an unexpected blessing or outcome. God's perspective is not the same as the world's viewpoint or value system. How do your children humble you and change how you view what's important? _I am so selfish. The more I cling_

to selfishness the worse mother I am. The more I strive to be
selfless, the happier I am.

How can these scriptures help you change your perspective?

Focus on His promises. The hard work of truly following Him
will pay off.

Which Beatitude do you identify with most currently and why? _vs. 8. Blessed are the pure of heart. Its what I_

strive for most.

Read James 1:2-6. Struggles appear to be the opposite of joy, but God wants us to view each challenge we face as a joy as it helps develop character. What has a recent struggle taught you? *Other than daily Jojo's allergies - eating well + taking care of our bodies.*

The Apostle Paul went through many struggles, including imprisonment. Read Philippians 1:12-15, 18. He reframed the problems into positive opportunities. How can you reframe one struggle to focus on the possibility for good?

The struggle of waking up in the middle of the night with Haddie. Enjoying her while she's still a baby.

Read Matthew 5:13-14. These verses follow the Beatitudes and remind us that our lives show people our faith. How can finding blessings of the Beatitudes help your faith shine? *Letting go of the world. Following what God calls us contradicts what the world tells us.*

When you think you are lacking in talent, or do not measure up to a certain expectation you have in mind, and or think you are not a good enough mother, remember God loves you and gave you a mother's heart. His Word says,

> *For we are God's masterpiece. He has created us anew in Christ Jesus, so we can do the good things he planned for us long ago.* EPHESIANS 2:10 NLT

Look at your sleeping child tonight and then write about how you love your child _Joanna, Naomi, and Haddie. Their smiles and laughter light my heart. Their hugs warm me. They are kind and sweet. Tenacious and silly. Adventurous and brave._

Stress Relievers

- Call a cheer-filled friend
- Take a long bath
- Walk or sit outside
- Simplify life
    - Keep less toys out and put the rest up to swap in a week or so.
    - Ease up on the calendar with a few nos.
    - Be more accepting of mistakes and less than perfection.
    - Have a few easy meal ideas and ingredients on hand for busy days.

Blessed is the mother who discovers joy in
each day, for she will smile as she rises.
Pause at the end of the day and
thank God for each blessing

Panic Prayers

Use a favorite scripture when you start to panic or say a simple prayer like this one:

Lord, you are with me in this mess. Calm my heart and guide me one step at a time to deal with this situation.

DAY 2

Imperfect Parents

Have I not commanded you? Be strong and courageous! Do not be terrified nor dismayed, for the Lord your God is with you wherever you go. JOSHUA 1:9

Left Behind

Even though we try our best, as parents we make mistakes. Here's my story.

I rushed back home when I found out my son James forgot to obey me and put his costume in the car for a school event. Back home, I yelled, "Everyone, stay in the car." I jumped out, raced to the door, ran downstairs, and grabbed the two-feet tall, bright yellow bird costume made with several plucked feather dusters.

I drove back to the school and asked James a question. When he didn't answer, I jokingly asked if he had lost his tongue or wasn't in the car.

Michael calmly stated, "He isn't here."

"Well, where is he?"

"He got out at home."

I checked behind me in the rearview mirror and then slammed on the brakes and twisted my head around. I panicked when I realized I'd left him at home.

I dropped the others off. My daughter Darlene glanced up, her lips quivered, and she whispered, "How can I be Little Bird without my Big Bird?"

My heart melted a tiny bit. "I'm going to get Big Bird."

I felt guilty, a failure for not counting noses before driving off. At home I saw James sitting on the front step. He explained that he had gone to the bathroom.

I questioned, "Were you scared when you came out and saw the car gone?"

My heart finished melting when I listened to his soft voice state, "No. You came back for my costume, so I knew you would come for me."

My son's words melted my heart. I realized his faith in me kept him calm. I needed more faith in God to remain calm. What has helped you be calm when things go wrong?

Going to God is the only answer.

Mary and Joseph Also Lost Their Son Jesus

We are not perfect, and neither were many people in the Bible. Mary and Joseph lost their son while traveling with extended family. The story is in Luke chapter 2 although we often skip that to focus on Luke 2:52 about Jesus growing in wisdom and stature. Outcomes are important but hassles are part of the journey. We often recall those panic moments, so we'll start with Mary stating the panic she and Joseph experienced.

Good Plans that Fall Apart

> *His parents didn't know what to think. "Son," his mother said to him, "why have you done this to us? Your father and I have been frantic, searching for you everywhere."* LUKE 2:48 NLT

Read Luke 2:41-45. What had Mary and Joseph planned and what really happened? How did Mary feel?

They thought Jesus was with but He had stayed behind.

Read Luke 2:46-50. How did Jesus derail the travel and family time plans? He left them and stayed behind.

How did Mary react to Jesus' change of plans?

Terrified. She viewed it as losing her son. She didn't understand what He meant.

How did outsiders view Jesus? They were amazed at His questions and understanding.

How did Jesus respond when they went home?

Soft reminder of His true purpose.

Parent's Nightmare

Mary and Joseph lost their son for three days and nights. They hunted everywhere and retraced their steps. This probably caused stress and frantic, sleepless nights. In Luke 2:49 Mary questioned Jesus about *why had He treated them that way* and *whether He didn't know they were worried*. This took place openly, in front of leaders. It revealed that Jesus did not have his parents' permission for his actions.

Jesus responded with a question that focused on God's will rather than circumstances. When has a child said something profound that caused you to rethink what's important?

Hold onto the "Mommy hold mes". I won't get to
hear them for much longer.

When have you used questions to get your children to think about their actions?

_1 24-7_

When have you publicly discussed a problem and when have you talked in private?

Not there yet

Read Luke 2:51-52. As parents, we see unity in Mary and Joseph. What happened as Jesus grew?

_____

In what ways do you and your spouse have unity in parenting?

Constantly talking and asking about what to do.

How do you recover when you feel you lost your cool or overreacted? What helps you calm down?

Realizing I've sinned and repenting.

The night after leaving James behind, we had a family talk and went over rules and the need to obey us. What helps your children obey you?

R-E-S-P-E-C-T. Why obey if they don't respect us?

Nightmare Moments

What happened that felt like a nightmare?

Naomi carrying Haddie by the neck and leaving the basement door open for her to almost fall down.

How did you react and then respond?

Yelled and got Haddie to safety.

How was the problem resolved?

Baby gates and explaining why not to grab around the neck.

What did you learn, and what did you teach your child? How are you coping? Or, if the situation is ongoing, who is giving you support?

To stop being too careless. It's not cool parenting, it can get deadly fast. Be vigilant. Watchful. Careful.

Obedience: A Key to Peace in the Home and Helping Our Children Thrive

Our children, unlike Jesus, are not God. It's not so simple to get them to obey continually. Peace and the desire to please God and their parents starts in their hearts as they accept Jesus into their lives.

ABCs of Faith

As parents, you guide your children. Moms and dads are the first ones to teach them about faith. Here are some basics thoughts to teach.

Admit that you disobey (sin) and know Jesus will forgive you (1 John 2:12)

Believe Jesus came and died for you. (John 3:16)

Call on God to become His child (John 1:12)

Scriptures and Obedience of Children

Read Ephesians 6:1-4. What balance does a parent need in training a child?

Disciplining without provoking to anger.

What promise should children learn about obeying God?

Obey your parents for it pleases the LORD.

Read Proverbs 22:6. What benefit comes from disciplining children?

When they are older, they will not depart.

Read Hebrews 12:5-11. What connection is made between discipline and love?

God disciplines us in love to train us up in righteousness. We should do the same. "Even our earthly fathers discipline us and we respected them for it.

Discipline and training can also be compared to learning a skill such as playing an instrument or a sport. What does it take to learn a skill?

Practice, practice, practice.

Practice matters too and that includes making mistakes and trying again. Read 1 Corinthians 9:24-27. Compare Paul's words about athletic discipline and training to learning behavior rules. How does that compare to following a rule?

Disciplining ourselves and mind in order to get our eternal prize. Doing so with self control.

A social child may think limiting social interaction/play dates is a big punishment, while a shy child may consider that a relief and reward. How do you respond to disobedience according to the action and/or to your child's personality?

Studying their personality. Getting to know/seeking out their heart.

What are benefits for children who are well behaved and learned to follow rules?

They will live long in the land God gives them. It pleases the LORD. I am less stressed.

Personality Chart

Consider each child's personality and a few ideas to guide them according to their bent. There's more on personalities later in the book.

Prayer

Read Psalm 139, and be thankful for God forming your child and knowing him or her so well. Use the Psalm to create a simple prayer like the following:

Lord, you formed and know my child. Help me to be understanding and respond according to my child's needs.

JoJo

Nay?

Type	Social Interactor	Powerful Director	Thoughtful Analyzer	Friendly Supporter
Characteristics	Talkative, likes attention, lacks focus	Bossy, goal oriented, gets things done, learns fast	Quiet, likes alone time, sensitive, may be artistic, likes to please you	Laid-back, procrastinates, witty, peacemaker
Motivated by	Fun, social rewards, show and tell after completing work	Give child choices and let them be in control of something small	Order, quiet time	Rest periods, peace, snacks
Study habits	Likes a study buddy, praise, and some fun elements, refocus child as needed	Will set goals, wants to choose curriculum, want applause for doing their work	Wants time to work, needs to lower expectations, and wants parent to appreciate their hard work	Schedule frequent breaks, set goals of a few steps/problems at a time, reward for finishing (jokes, rest, snack)
Desk area	Place desk in a high traffic area	Mount a bulletin board for charts, goals	Set up in a quiet, private area, with containers to keep things organized	Avoid a chair that's too comfy, set up where child can see, help child refocus on completing tasks
Devotions	Act it out, focus on Bible people, stories, and hands-on fun	Focus on action, point out what worked, hands on activities with a purpose	Dig into questions, look at maps, charts, artistic activities that illustrate facts	Simple chat, see how Bible people achieved peace

DAY 3

Work, Joy, and Balance

*I know that there is nothing better for
them than to rejoice and to do good in
one's lifetime.* ECCLESIASTES 3:12

Mother's Day

Rhonda dreamed of a perfect day with all the clothes
washed, folded, and put away, and a clean kitchen. Her little children laughed at the thought. They could not do that.

So, she chose to choose joy. She took the children outside with lots of bubbles and wands, and toys. They pic-
nicked and snapped photos all afternoon, made their own
peanut butter and jelly sandwiches with no inside mess,
but lots of laughter. She enjoyed the feast day with celebrating and food they liked.

Sometimes our dreams of perfection need to give way
to reality and simpler plans that bring joy.

A King's Answer to Work and Balance

Wise King Solomon asked God to give him a wise and understanding heart (2 Chronicles 1:1-12). He used his wisdom to make good decisions and guide the people. He contemplated the good and need for work and pleasure. We need balance. Solomon's wisdom in Ecclesiastes reminds us to be balanced.

> *What do we gain by all of our hard work? I have seen what difficult things God demands of us. God makes everything happen at the right time. Yet none of us can ever fully understand all he has done, and he puts questions in our minds about the past and the future.* ECCLESIASTES 3:9-11 CEV

Solomon, who had many wives and children, penned the above words of choosing joy in the face of busywork.

How much of your daily work simply keeps you busy, and what parts do you consider ministry?

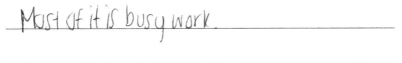

Most of it is busy work.

How often have you cleaned something only to have little hands quickly mess it up again and then wondered why you made the effort?

Almost all day.

Have you ever felt like you see little results from efforts on a daily basis? How do you see growth when you compare months or years? _Never on a daily basis._

~~xxxx~~ ~~xxxx~~ Rarely a month. Mostly I see

growth over the year.

We don't see *full* results of raising children for years. Motherhood starts with labor and continues with more labor. We see steps of growth along the way from growing taller and gaining abilities, to increasing in knowledge and understanding.

_____

_____

How have you considered the labor of motherhood a gift?

I have the blessing of watching them grow.
My toil brings them joy.

Mealtimes

Solomon continued his writing with the thought that it is good to enjoy the time we have:

> *I know that there is nothing better for them than to rejoice and to do good in one's lifetime; moreover, that every person who eats and drinks sees good in all his labor—this is the gift of God.* ECCLESIASTES 3:12-13

Moms spend lots of time providing snacks and meals. Eating and drinking are a big part of family life. So is cleanup but leave that for another day and use paper plates today. Let your children help clean.

How can you enjoy mealtime?

Simple, healthy meals that taste wonderful.
Ignoring all the dishes.

How do you savor the crunching and munching sounds of your children and the smiles when they have full tummies? Do you look at them and listen and talk while sitting together? What are your favorite topics?

Beginning to talk to them about Jesus, I love when
they enjoy my cooking and labor.

Read Matthew 15:32. Jesus had compassion for hungry people. Some days when children grumble and whine, they just need food and compassion. How do you respond to your tired, hungry children?

I usually snap. Mostly because I am just as
hungry and tired.

Sometimes food fights or spills happen. Sometimes dinner burns or we discover we're missing a main ingredient. Those are times to laugh at the mistakes and be creative.

What has been your worst meal disaster?

Anything coconutty totally flops.

How did you respond? Did you recover? If so, how?

I tend to take it really hard. It hurts when they don't enjoy my cooking.

Reasons for Meals

Studies show more and more that mealtimes are very important in raising children. The kitchen table is the hub of life. At meals we share our giggles and tears, discuss events, explain future plans, and enjoy being together. When children are satisfied and relaxed it's easier to discuss behavior and problems.

There are so many reasons for sharing meals including handling stress, conversation, bonding, nurturing, celebrating and thanking God for the blessings of food, healthy eating, and sharing our days and realizing how God worked in our lives.

Read the following groups of scriptures, and describe the benefits of those meals or foods.

Genesis 2:9 (note that the Hebrew word for good is *towb* and means the best of the best).

good trees for food. Delicious, healthy, natural food. Basically fruit is the best.

Exodus 16:12, Deuteronomy 12:7, Isaiah 1:19

God provides. We rejoice in His blessings, We provides

more when we're obedient.

Leviticus 23:16, 24; Ecclesiastes 3:13, 9:7; John 2:1-2

offering to the LORD. , eat and take pleasure in our toil.

Matthew 15:32, 37-38

Lose faith over starvation? Again, God provides.

Luke 14:1-6, Luke 22:19, John 21:12-14

Psalm 104:14-15, Luke 19:1-10

John 2:3-11

Make Meals Fun

- Use words of praise, not complaint or scolding while eating together.
- Let children join in setting and clearing the table to develop a sense of belonging.
- Find something to laugh at with meals or snacks, even making silly faces.
- Use mealtime to explain plans for later (later that day or even the next day's plans).
- Mention the nutrition of various foods of the meal and how it helps our muscles grow strong, our skin glow, and our eyes sparkle.
- Have a new healthy food to try once a week and talk about its nutritional value.
- Share the best of the day and cheer for each person. Share the tough parts too, and empathize with each one; plus guide children in what might make things better next time.

What have been successful meals for you? What will you work on to improve your mealtimes?

More family time. Less stress.

Prayer

Lord, help me prepare healthy meals and snacks. Give me the strength to cook and wisdom on what I buy and serve. Help my children appreciate the healthier foods.

DAY 4

Routines and Plans

God is not a God of confusion, but of peace. 1 Corinthians 14:33

Simplifying Life

Organization works out better with plans and being prepared to carry them out. I am not a morning person, so I always work out my plans in the evening and prepare things ahead. I make lists of what to do in the morning. That makes my life easier. My children learned to check the posted dinner menu for the month rather than ask what's for supper. My kids knew I checked the backpacks at night. They also knew their own morning routine to get ready for the day. Our homelife always ran smoother with team effort.

As moms, we should make plans during our peak hours. What are your peak hours?

Night time

How do you use those peak hours?

Typically snacking or on my phone.

What is your biggest organizational challenge? What might help?

Too much stuff. Purges. The morning adventures are always chaotic. Packing lunches or making coffee. Prepping breakfast ahead. Especially Haddie's.

Thinking Ahead (Luke 14:28-34)

Jesus spoke about plans in relation to a decision to construct a building. He cautioned people to count the cost before starting a project.

For moms, plans can change quickly, but they still help guide our days and give children a sense of routine and what to expect. Counting the time to prepare, travel, and gather supplies needs to be done ahead of scheduling an activity or before an event.

Read Luke 14:28-34.

Restate what Jesus said about planning ahead before building a tower or facing an opponent.

Count the cost, see if you have enough to finish it. If you do not have enough you will be mocked and foolish.

What is your purpose when you make plans for cleaning your home, meals, or an outing?

To serve my family and bring them joy.

What must be considered in supplies, preparations, and time needed for plans such as menus and housework?____

Time. Paper, pens, cookbooks, quiet time, right attitude, directions, anything prepped ahead be prepped ahead.

When something interrupts, we can consider it a redirection from God. Read Proverbs 16:3, 9. How can you commit your plans to God?

Prayer prayer prayer. Submission. A willing heart to hand over my "job"

When has God allowed an interruption of plans to be a way to redirect you?

I can't think of mine. He redirected Beth's plans for a date to be able to share the gospel with Chris.

Read Psalm 37:3-5 and Proverbs 3:5-7.

As moms, it's good to establish routines and plans. What are some routines that make your life easier?

Prepping the night before. Cleaning the night before. Leaving the morning for exercise and time with God.

When does chaos break out? What routine could help you keep order at those times?

_____

_____

Bag of Tricks to Help Plans Succeed

It might be nice to be a magician who could wave a wand and make a mess disappear. Instead, create a bag of tricks to keep an energetic child from creating unplanned problems.

Store small toys that are favorites in a large bag or container. Then, take out one to occupy his or her energy so you can focus on a task. This recycles toys and keeps them as special treats.

Call for God's help

Read Psalm 90:12-17 (also read it in the Message version). This psalm is a prayer, one that moms might echo many times. What does it call for God to do?

_____

_____

What will a reminder of God's love do for your day?

_____

_____

How does this prayer show the hope that God's plans help us survive the hard moments?

_____

_____

Even housework can be done for God. How has God affirmed your efforts to make your home a happy, clean, and safe place?

_____

_____

Read Ephesians 5:15-16. *Be careful* is a reminder to think of safety first. How has rushing caused accidents?

_____

_____

_____

The Message version calls these desperate times at the end of verse 16. When have you felt desperate?

_____

_____

How can you make even bad moments teachable ones and thus make the most of opportunities?

_____

_____

How do plans help you keep a more balanced life amid a life that is full of busyness?

_____

_____

_____

Scripture Tips for Planning

Read Jeremiah 29:11. What does God remind you about His plans?

_____

_____

Read Proverbs 16:3. Before planning, what do you do?

_____

_____

Instead of filling up the calendar and cramming it with things you think you or your children need to do, consider simpler plans. There are more seasons ahead; there's no not need to go into time debt. What are the most important goals to reach now for you and for your children?

_____

_____

_____

What routines do you have for children?

_____

_____

_____

How do routines help?

_____

_____

_____

Full Days

It might seem that children have so much energy that they must have found a way to siphon it from their parents into their tanks. They undo hours of efforts in seconds if you turn your back or don't cut them off at the passage of freshly cleaned areas.

Routines

Children adapt to routines. Consider scheduling a set time each day for your housework, such as laundry. Let children become accustomed to helping or playing quietly when you are working, with the reward of mommy time when the scheduled time ends (we know the work doesn't really end). A chart for routines helps children remember each step. Little ones can have a picture chart.

Times When Routines Simplify Life

- Mornings (grooming, dressing, eating)
- Preparing to leave the house
- Meals
- Bedtime

Be Flexible

To make the most of everyone's time, make daily plans and routines, but don't be surprised if little ones and emergencies run interference. Instead, build in time cushions (short breaks) to handle the problems. And when plans go smoothly, enjoy the time cushion by spending it with your little ones.

Prayer

Pray for wisdom and understanding as Solomon did in 1 Kings 3:6-9.

DAY 5

Little Night Terrorists

He caused the storm to be still, so that the
waves of the sea were hushed. Psalm 107:29

For a few months my children appeared to work together on *Operation Deprive Mom of Sleep.* Each one took a different hour or two during the night to wake me up. Every hour, a little one cried, jumped on me, or stood and breathed on me, wanting my attention. I felt like I had a small military patrol and the soldiers had joined forces and laid out a well-planned strategy. I was no match for them.

I tried the normal routines of providing drinks beside beds, nightlights, comforting stuffed friends, and more to help them survive a night in bed. Still, they persisted in wanting me even if I couldn't open my eyes, talk coherently, and stumbled my way to helping them. Becky, age six, even drilled me with commands, "Mom, you need to open the juice can first" or "Turn on the water" or "Turn off the water NOW." I tried to bargain with God for a few hours of rest to no avail.

Each morning, Becky would arrive, throw open the curtains, and yell, "Mom it's a brand-new day."

I'd try to lift my eyelids and peek out to see if I could focus. Nope, it was hard to focus without sleep. I groaned and tried to sleep in, but Becky would round up her little siblings, carry in the baby, and they'd all make it clear they needed me.

I prayed for help. God continually turned me to 2 Corinthians 12:9 to let me know His grace was sufficient. I complained that I needed sleep. Finally, I cried out, "Then I need your time for sleep to be sufficient." I gave my nights to God and asked Him to give me all the sleep I needed. From that time on, I awoke refreshed no matter how many hours, or how few minutes I slept.

When have you had sleepless night or tiring days?

_____

_____

What helps and what refreshes you?

_____

_____

Read Psalm 4:8. Have you prayed for the Lord to give you rest?

_____

_____

Years ago, when I could not sleep even when my children slept, I asked God to give me the name of someone who needed prayer. He did. I prayed and then fell asleep. I discovered that praying for someone takes my mind off my problems and helps me relax. God always gives me someone's name for whom I can pray. When I mentioned to that person that I prayed for her (or him), I often discover they needed prayer at that time.

Try it. When you cannot sleep ask God to name someone for whom you can pray. Write what happens.

_____

_____

_____

Jesus and a Sleepless Night (Mark 14:32-42)

The night before His death, Jesus stayed awake when He was grieved and distressed. He prayed and tried to get His sleepy friends to pray. He prayed three times, asking above all, for God's will to be done. Then He woke his friends and stated that the hour had come for Him to be betrayed.

Have you ever lain awake unable to sleep and simply prayed? _____

_____

_____

_____

Read Matthew 11:28. How do your little ones seem like night terrors causing weariness?

_____

_____

In reality, little ones are afraid of the dark, the separation, and need reassurance to rest peacefully.

What can you do to give children nighttime peace and rest from fear?

_____

_____

_____

Read Psalm 91. God tells us not to fear the night terrors and that means little ones too. What other comforting thoughts on rest are in the Psalm 91?

_____

_____

_____

Read Matthew 11:28 again. Motherhood can be a tiring job. What does Jesus promise us?

_____

_____

_____

At night how do you unwind?

_____

_____

Read 1 Peter 5:7. When has prayer, and giving your worries to God helped?

_____

_____

Types of Rest

Dr. Saundra Smith identified seven types of rest we need.

- Physical rest of sleep that lets the body recover
- Mental rest to relax your thoughts and let go of worries and fears
- Sensory rest from too many electronics, noise, and stimulation to your eyes, ears, and other senses
- Emotional rest from stress, emotional outbursts, and our relationships that drain us.
- Creative rest from new ideas, thoughts, and solutions
- Social rest from social activities
- Spiritual rest from faith events

Each type of rest refreshes us in a different way to help us be energized, at peace, quiet within, less stressed, more creative, relaxed, and renewed in our souls. That gives us hope that we can enjoy our days. Let's look these up in the Bible to find solutions that help to bring us total rest.

Physical rest

Read Hebrews 4:9-10 and Exodus 23:12. The word used for rest or ceased is *katepausen*. It means to cease or rest. It refers to stopping all work. How does that help you consider how to rest physically?

_____

Is there a place you can sit without seeing tools or a mess? Perhaps you need to make such a little spot to sit and reenergize.

_____

_____

Mental rest

Read Philippians 4:8-9 and Isaiah 26:3. If your mind dwells on problems and negative thoughts, there's no rest mentally. How do these verses share ideas for peace of mind for mental rest?

_____

_____

Read Mark 4:19. This is a verse from the parable of the sower. How are worries, riches, and other things distractions from keeping a calm mind?

_____

_____

Sometimes it helps to write out the problems, pray over them, and then toss out the paper to let go and give it to God. What else helps you release your mental stress?

Sensory rest

Read Mark 6:31-32. Where did Jesus lead His friends at a time of grief (death of John the Baptist) when they were surrounded by crowds with no time to eat? How does this remind you to retreat when you are overwhelmed by noise, sights, and electronics?

Where do you have a quiet place to retreat?

Emotional rest

When anxiety, fear, and other emotions rob you of peace, you cannot rest easy. Read Philippians 4:6-7 and John 14:27. Scriptures remind us to let go and let the Lord guard your heart. Pray now and give any emotional feelings to God and the problem that caused emotional upheaval.

When the emotions are caused by people, especially people we interact with daily, it helps to set boundaries. That might mean a timer for how long a person can speak or certain hours the person must leave you alone (if they are old enough). What can you try to create emotional rest time?

_____

_____

_____

Read Matthew 8:24, and notice what happened as Jesus slept. He trusted the Father and had no fear. How can you increase your trust when you are afraid? Read Matthew 8:25-27, and consider what Jesus said as you answer.

_____

_____

_____

Creative rest

Read Genesis 2:2-3. God spent six days in full creativity mode. Then what did He do?

_____

_____

Studies, including one out of the University of York and University of Florida found that 40 percent of creative ideas come after we rest our minds, such as taking breaks.

Letting your mind relax also inspires creativity. When have you been the most creative?

_____

_____

Social rest

Jesus loves people and yet He often withdrew after being surrounded by crowds. Read Matthew 14:23, Mark 1:45, and Luke 5:15-16. Jesus took time to pray that would help Him refocus on God. When we only please people we can forget our call and what God wants. When have you felt tired from being around people (including your own children)?

_____

_____

For moms, that break may only come when your little children sleep. If so, don't use that time for work, but pray and rest quietly or soak in a bath. What helps you relax when you're alone?

_____

_____

Spiritual rest

It's hard to think we need spiritual rest. Don't we always want to be connected with God? Yet, ask a preacher or minister how they feel after they minister or speak. They are usually drained from the energy expended. Read Psalm 23:1-3 and Psalm 46:10. How are these scriptures reminders that God knows our souls also need refreshing and renewal?

_____

_____

_____

What do you do to refresh your soul?

_____

_____

Children also need all those types of rest. They can be surrounded by toys and people to a point of over-stimulation. They can play hard and need sleep. They can also be afraid to sleep because they fear shadows or being alone in the dark. What helps your child rest in each way needed?

_____

_____

_____

What interests' help your children let go of worries and relax?

_____

_____

Nighttime Bag of Tricks

- If needed, use a nightlight to remind your children that Jesus is with them. Teach them to look at the light and talk or sing to Jesus, the light of the world (John 8:12).
- Engage in quiet activities before bedtime.
- Pray with your child for a restful sleep.
- Consider letting your child have a cup of water nearby to drink.
- Create a short routine (brushing teeth, story, cuddling, lullaby, prayer, kiss) to help children quietly transition to sleep.
- Be firm about sending a child back to bed if he or she gets up.
- Nightmares may follow a scary event, like overhearing an argument, scary movie, or other stress. Talk the problems of the day through before bedtime.
- Care for needs but avoid cuddling a child who wakes up during the night, as that pleasure could cause them to repeatedly wake up. Instead, offer a stuffed animal to snuggle with them.

A Mother's End-of-the-Day Scripture Prayer:

Generous in love—God, give grace! Huge in mercy—wipe out my bad record. Scrub away my guilt, soak out my sins in your laundry. I know how bad I've been; my sins are staring me down. Amen. PSALM 51:1-3 [MSG]

Then read verse 10 in a different translation.

WEEK 2

A Home with a Little Organization

Weeks in *Growing a Mother's Heart*
that coordinate with this week's study

Week 16: Creating a Haven

Week 23: Balancing Act
and a Simpler Life

Note: If you are super organized and have a home
that stays looking great, consider encouraging
a friend who has a hard time with organization.
Let this section inspire you with ideas on how
to help and add your own tips to share.

DAY 1

Look at How I helped!

The wise woman builds her house, but the foolish tears it down with her own hands. PROVERBS 14:1

We moved to Florida with five children, so unpacking and getting organized seemed daunting. I marked boxes before we moved that indicated where they belonged in the new home. For each bedroom, I marked whether the contents contained clothes for a dresser, closet, or bookcase, and whether toys went onto shelves, into the closet, or into a toy box.

The day after the movers left, my six-year-old daughter Darlene rushed down the stairs yelling, "Come! Look at how I helped! I unpacked everything."

I followed and stared into her room. She had dumped the contents of every box onto the floor. Marbles, dolls, and upturned books lay scattered among underwear, dresses, and markers. So much for my system of unpacking one box at a time in her room, to store things in the proper places. I quickly grabbed the clothes to keep them from wrinkling. I gave her an empty box to put all her dolls in.

I gave her a second box to put in broken items and things she no longer wanted.

The doorbell rang. My organized sister-in-law arrived, and Darlene couldn't wait to show her how she had unpacked. She smiled and encouraged Darlene as they discussed what Darlene should do. Then she left the room and exploded with laughter.

Children can quickly derail plans and turn things into chaos. Sometimes we need a plan B and a sense of humor.

———————

Think of a time you faced your worst mess. Describe it:

_____

_____

_____

How have your children added to disorder when they tried to help?

_____

_____

Read Proverbs 14:1 again. How does a woman build a home and what causes a home to fall apart?

_____

_____

_____

How, as a woman, are you responsible for order in your home?

_____

_____

_____

How do your children and spouse help? Does everyone have assigned chores?

_____

_____

_____

We know some of the challenges of disorder, especially how much easier items get lost. One motivated woman in the Bible set about to find a lost item, a coin.

Lost and Found (Based on Luke 15:8-10)

In The Parable of the Lost Coin, a woman sweeps the floor to find her coin. If there was a longer version, we'd know she had to take care of the pile of laundry and toys on the floor before she could sweep. She probably picked up more items too and had to find places to put everything. In effect, she had to get organized before she could sweep and find the lost coin.

When I start cleaning, I find lost objects. If I keep the house organized, objects don't get lost, and I save lots of time. If I make sure the children do their part in staying organized, we all save time and frustration.

When have you lost something because of clutter?

_____

_____

When has organization helped you locate items or papers easily? What helped the most?

_____

_____

What do you lose most often, and what might prevent that loss? At one time I continually misplaced keys. I ended up putting them on a stretch bracelet and kept it on until I was at the hook for my keys and hung them up.

_____

_____

Roadblocks to Being Organized

Grief, problems, and even learning disabilities like ADD can be additional roadblocks to organizing. What are your biggest challenges in getting organized?

_____

_____

We need self-care, so be sure to take time to deal with your emotional needs. Anger, grief, and other feelings can immobilize us. What are you doing to take care of your needs?

_____

_____

How can you overcome the challenges?

_____

_____

What motivates you? How can you use your motivation to start organizing things?

_____

_____

Understand your personality to know more about what motivates you. Here's a quick guide:

- **Social Interactor (like Peter)**
  - This is someone who loves to party, talk, and be with others. This person does not focus as easily but is motivated by the promise of socializing. So, promise yourself you can party with your children or a friend once you complete your task or goal.
- **Powerful Director (like Paul)**
  - An extroverted born leader wants to be in control, sets goals, and accomplishes a lot. This mom wants respect and approval for their accomplishments. They tend to be self-motivated with their

own goals. Enlisting children to cheer when things are organized reaffirms your efforts.

- **Thoughtful Analyzer (like Priscilla)**
  - — This mom is an introvert who thinks deeply, analyzes information, strives for perfection, wants order, proceeds with caution (slow to make decisions), and prefers to be with only a few people at a time. They will persist if praised instead of receiving complaints. They motivate themselves by posting positive mottos and their own need to be organized. They hinder things when they are too self-critical and expectations are too high. So lower your expectations to reality and accept a level of children's natural disorder.

- **Friendly Supporter (like Mary, sister of Lazarus)**
  - — This is the amiable, diplomatic mom with a good sense of humor who prefers relaxed settings and tends to procrastinate. Motivate yourself with promise of relaxation, peace, or time to share jokes and stories.

Tips to Organization

What is your personality. What motivates you?

_____

_____

_____

One big step is to have a place for everything and keep items in their places. What items have no place and where can you make a place for those objects?

For children, you can use labels as a reminder of where things should be kept. What do you do when your children have trouble keeping organized?

Read 1 Corinthians 14:40. Getting organized means having a plan of what to do and when to do it. Sometimes that's focusing on one spot a day or scheduling certain tasks on specific days such as what day to wash floors and which days to do laundry. What do you schedule, or will you start to schedule?

Beyond the Cleaning

Remember the woman who found her lost coin? What did she do once she found her lost coin?

Yes, she celebrated. She had a clean home once she found the coin, so she could invite people to come and party. Part of balance is to take time to rejoice, be hospitable, and enjoy friendships.

_____

_____

How have you been hospitable?

_____

_____

How have you celebrated with your children when you all worked to clean the house?

_____

_____

It can be good to go outside with bubbles or to a park to keep the house clean. List a few ways to celebrate with children that will not create a new mess:

_____

_____

_____

Good Organizational Habits for Kids

- Put things away when finished with them as quickly as possible.

- Stick with cleaning once you start.
- Look at your room each day and notice what needs to be cleaned.
- Make sure you have a place for everything and put items in the right place.
- Don't let distractions stop you from your tasks.
- Trust your choices, including getting rid of what you no longer need.
- Don't say yes if you don't have time for a new activity.
- Take a picture when the room looks great and post it to remember you can clean it!

Read Lamentations 3:22-23

The good news is that every day gives us a fresh start. Praise God for fresh mercy and also ask the Lord to help you extend mercy to your children and let them know it's a new day that the Lord has made!

Pray

Thanks, Lord, for the blessings of motherhood and for each child you gave me. Give me the strength and wisdom to be more organized today and more relaxed. Let me also laugh when a child makes a mess, and then help guide them to clean up.

DAY 2

Chaos and Order
in the Bible

*The earth was a shapeless, chaotic mass,
with the Spirit of God brooding over the dark
vapors. Then God said, "Let there be light."
And light appeared.* GENESIS 1:2-3 TLB

Little Tornadoes

Children can blow through a room like a fast-moving tornado. I recall returning from an evening out with my husband to see the biggest mess ever as the teen babysitter
failed to keep any order. Toys were dumped everywhere,
pillows lay on the floor with crumbs and drinks spilled
on them, and the mess continued. It's a familiar scene for
many moms. And the children were all still awake. I sent
them off to bed and told the sitter to come by the next day
for some tips.

The sitter had lost her mother at a young age, and I
believed God wanted me to guide her. My energetic children were a challenge for me let alone an inexperienced

teen. The children spent the next day cleaning up the mess they made, my husband worked on removing stains (he did the laundry), and I gathered and put the items that caused the biggest mess into storage as a punishment. Consequences for disobeying rules make the best teachers.

The teen showed up fearing she'd been a big failure, but I told her my kids failed us both. I shared ideas on how to control them and gave her a loaf of freshly baked bread. I taught her to make bread over several weeks while sharing tips. She became a very sought-after sitter.

God Understands Chaos (Genesis 1)

God looked and saw chaos, so the story began. He started with light that revealed everything.

I have learned to follow His example and start with prayer to enlighten me.

When facing new challenges, I research or ask wiser moms to enlighten me. I also follow his pattern of how He created order.

What orderly method did God choose? Did He multitask or focus on one task at a time?

_____

_____

_____

What was God's order for creation?

_____

_____

Read Isaiah 45:18. What plans did God have for the earth? What did He not create it to be?

_____

_____

Read 1 Corinthians 14:40. Note the verse said *all things* must be done properly and in an orderly manner. How does it help to keep on a schedule and routines?

_____

_____

God's Vision

God had a vision and a plan. He created beauty one step at a time and focused on one thing at a time from creating light, plants, and creatures to creating people. It made sense to make water and sunshine before plants, etc. God's plans included putting everything in place.

He understood one of the first rules of change: We change either:

1. because we reach rock bottom that forces us to face reality and change; or

2. we have a vision of what could be that draws us to work toward a goal.

What motivator do you prefer?

_____

_____

_____

When have you reached a goal because of a vision?

_____

_____

Visions help so much! Write your vision as a goal or post a photo that reflects your dream.

_____

_____

_____

Read 1 Corinthians 14:33 again.

Some translations use the word confusion or breach while others use disorder. It refers to order within the church. It also reveals something about the nature of God and order. How is order related to peace?

_____

_____

When the home is organized, it helps nurture peace and tranquility. When has your chaos added to unrest and lack of peace?

_____

_____

A vision helps us move toward a goal. What is your vision for your home and the organization in your home?

_____

_____

Points to Remember When Organizing

1. Start with a vision of what you really want.
2. Commitment is essential.
3. Organizing is a process, not a one-time effort.
4. Creating beauty is the highest goal of organizing.
5. Decide what you need to make the vision a reality and how to get it.
6. Be specific. Write the vision and steps to reach it out. Generalities seldom work.
7. You must put forth effort. Just thinking won't do it.
8. Avoid perfectionism. Just do it.
9. Get outside help where possible.
10. Realize that organizing is a part of your maturing.

Reward Yourself for Success (or Big Steps)

A Few Keys to Organized Living

Read Ephesians 5:16, and consider how to change how you spend time.

Read how Abraham asked Sarah to make bread with fine flour when unexpected visitors appeared in Genesis 18:6. He also ran off to prepare meat. Sara did this. That meant she had finely ground flour, along with other ingredients plus time to drop things and cook. That takes organization. This was before she became a mother.

Schedule Time Cushions

Read Psalm 23:1-2. I try to build in time cushions, little breaks throughout the day. These refresh me and also give me time for the unexpected, whether it's a friend dropping in or a problem that arises.

Read Ecclesiastes 3:1 about a time for everything. Trust God plans for enough days for your life and that you can choose how to fill the calendar.

How do you schedule your down time?

_____

_____

Read Proverbs 10:4 and 20:4. How do you counter laziness?

_____

_____

How is being lazy different from investing time in playing with your children?

_____

_____

Time Tips

- Keep a time diary for a few weeks to see how you really spend your time. Then start eliminating time wasters, and you'll have time to organize.
- Do a place check.
  - Save time by keeping items in their place. Check what items have specific places and what ones don't have a place (for example, items for mail, school supplies, craft supplies, sets of toys).
- Create routines and stick to them.
  - Set up rules on making beds and cleaning up toys for children. Tie it to a reward such as no snack until they complete the tasks or playing a game when the work is done.
- Make sure you schedule time for God. He needs to be a priority.

Prayer

Pray 1 Corinthians 14:33.

DAY 3

Too Much Stuff

There is a sickening evil which I have seen under the sun: wealth being hoarded by its owner to his detriment. ECCLESIASTES 5:13

Too Many Toys and Stuffed Animals, Too Little Space

My younger daughter saved everything and kept it all in her room. Items tumbled onto the floor, covered her bed and desk, and made it impossible to have space to play. One day I asked, "Would you like a beautiful room where you can find things?" She nodded. I shared some ideas for her to pick a few of my ideas to try.

She chose to help make extra shelves from covered cardboard boxes to hold lightweight items like small stuffed animals and little toys. She also agreed to fill a big plastic tub with items and switch them out every few months. It would be like opening a treasure box each time she swapped out items. She agreed to give away what she no longer needed and toss out broken toys. We also put all the teen dolls with clothes and accessories in a tub to keep in my closet. She could use them when she cleaned her room, but had to put them away before the day ended. That transformed her room.

Too Much Stuff for Biblical Relatives

We're not the first to juggle staying organized and having room for stuff or to deal with what happens when a person's hoarding takes priority over relationships. Let's check out what happened with an uncle and his nephew as they grew rich and amassed stuff.

Read Genesis chapter 13.

Read verses 6 and 9 again. What caused a problem between Abraham and Lot? What solution did they come up with?

_____

_____

Read Genesis 14:12-13 How did Abraham learn about Lot's plight? What does that reveal about their closeness after they separated?

_____

_____

Stuff Divided Family

Abraham rescued Lot and then and rescued Lot's possessions. Lot may even have lived with Abraham again at that time, but we know later Lot and his family lived in the city of Sodom.

Stuff is not necessarily bad. God blessed Solomon and showered him with wealth. Jesus was very generous. He fed people not a little, but abundantly. It's our priorities and attitudes that cause problems.

Do you fight over possessions in your family? Do things take on more value than people?

_____

_____

_____

Read Proverbs 24:3-4. Wisdom and understanding helps a woman organize the home. When toys overflowed the play area, I kept out some toys and stored others to not have too much stuff around. Rooms stayed more organized and rotating toys kept children from getting bored. What messes have you faced, and what advice helps you be organized?

_____

_____

_____

Read Matthew 15:33, 37. It always amazed me that, in a desolate, remote place the disciples had a dozen containers to store leftovers. Jesus gave them so much, and they shared it all, but He also blessed them with baskets of leftovers. Do you keep containers for storing things? How do you prepare for organizing new things or leftovers?

_____

_____

Are you blessed with lots of material possessions? How is that working for you?

_____

_____

Read Psalm 119:45. How does wisdom make a home a good place to live? What brings freedom?

_____

_____

_____

God's rules and precepts bring freedom. Precepts and other rules can help us in daily life. Lists, investing in containers, and other tools for order assist us. We want to build a home and not live in a pigsty or a heap of clutter.

Consider your ways. Do you follow the example of the woman in Proverbs 31:10-15 of making household responsibility a priority? Are you acting like the lazy person in Proverbs 15:19?

_____

_____

Simple Ideas for Home Organization

- Start in one corner of a room and move around, cleaning out clutter in one place at a time.
- Use a trash bag and a few containers as you work. Use one container to hold items to toss away, one for items to put back in their spots, and one for items to give away (duplicates, no longer needed).
- Take it easy. A little at a time is better than getting worn out by trying to do it all in one day.
  — Notice what area is too cluttered, and find new containers/homes for the items. If needed papers are piling up, get some folders and a holder for the folders.
- Label storage containers, and buy ones that will work.
  — If you need to see things, buy clear containers.
  — If you tend to just drop things as you go, then use baskets and attractive open storage bins to store items.
  — If you find you are cramming things anywhere, stop before putting something away and ask yourself where it really belongs. Start sorting items into specific places, and give more away.
- Look around your home and check the sore spots where things pile up. Think of ways to change those piles into something more organized with storage units, containers, or shelves.

Prayer

Pray for wisdom with Proverbs 3:5-6.

DAY 4

Distractions and Paper Chases

Then Hilkiah the high priest said to Shaphan the scribe, "I have found the Book of the Law in the house of the Lord." And Hilkiah gave the book to Shaphan, who read it. 2 KINGS 22:8

Hunt for Lost Items and Papers

"Mom, I can't find my passport," Darlene woke me up in the middle of the night after a frantic search she had made.

"Think about where you put it. You leave on your mission trip in a few hours," I said as I followed her to her room. I mentally thought of how I had asked her to place it in her suitcase a week earlier. I arrived at her room and stood a bit shocked to see the contents of drawers strewn onto the floor.

Tears streamed down her cheeks as she cried, "I know I have to leave. I know you told me to put it in my suitcase, but I never did. I looked everywhere. I thought I had it in my folder."

I started shuffling through the piles on her desk. I finally found the blue folder where I told her to keep important papers for the trip. I carefully turned one page at a time and found the passport in the middle of a booklet."

Darlene hugged me. We cleaned up.

Alas, we had a similar repeat problem when Darlene prepared for a tenth-wedding-anniversary trip.

I answered the phone to Darlene's frantic voice, "Mom, do you have my birth certificate? I can't find it. I think I was so worried I'd lose it that I never took it when I married. I forgot to renew my passport and we leave on our trip in a few days."

Darlene had spent a week at the house a month earlier, but she had never read what she needed to bring on her cruise until the day she called even though she had planned the trip nine months earlier. I opened the safe box and saw her birth certificate. I had to overnight it to ensure it would arrive in time.

Lost Book in the Bible

It's amazing how we can misplace some of our most important papers. Havoc reigns. We're not alone in losing papers. God's people lost the most valuable papers ever written. When King Josiah heard about the discovery of the scrolls by the priest, he tore his robes. He realized how its loss, the most important words they possessed, impacted their relationship with God.

The Lost Words of God

Read 2 Kings 22:9-11.

What did God's priests lose and finally find?

_____

_____

Josiah regretted the loss and created a plan to restore things according to God's Word. He made changes. How have you made changes after finding an important document that you lost?

_____

_____

What changes can you make to keep better track of papers like shot records, insurance, bills, your Bible study guide, and other documents?

_____

_____

Have you lost touch with God's Word? What can you do to read the Bible daily?

_____

_____

Read verse about sluggards: Proverbs 20:4, 21:25, and 24:30-34

What happens when you procrastinate?

_____

_____

Read Ecclesiastes 7:29. How do we complicate our lives? How do distractions or lack of attention to details add to problems?

_____

_____

_____

Read 1 Thessalonians 4:11-12 and Proverbs 31:10, 27-31. What are the rewards when you take your responsibilities seriously and care for your family and home?

_____

_____

_____

How do we let our stuff and plans distract us from the people we love? How does it help to have some easy meal plans or food on hand in case of unexpected company?

_____

_____

Consider Solomon's wise words

> *See, this alone I found: God made human*
> *beings straightforward, but they search for*
> *many complications.* ECCLESIASTES 7:29 CEB

What simple systems are working for you and when have complex ones caused problems? This may be as simple as a quilt or blanket instead of fancy bedding that makes it easy for a child to make a bed.

_____

_____

Filing System

It's important to handle papers when you get them or to put them where you can easily find them and complete the work at a time without distractions.

You may have a filing cabinet or not, but you should have storage and a system for keeping papers safe and easy to find. This might be a simple accordion folder with dividers, a three-ring binder with clear plastic sleeves to slide papers in and out. Or maybe you scan documents into a folder in your computer. What is your system, and how is it working out?

_____

_____

_____

Tips to Handle Papers Efficiently

Reads Proverbs 15:23 that shares about the importance of timely words. We need encouragement and sometimes that means encouraging ourselves with a motto or two.

- Try to handle a paper once (pay the bill, file the report, etc.).
- If you can't complete a task add a sticky note with a message about the next step to be done.
- Toss out junk mail and anything you no longer need, ASAP.
- File or scan documents you need to keep.
- Invest in a file cabinet or storage area for important papers.
- Consider paperless documents emailed to you and how to store them. Some companies keep them in accessible files for you to sign in and find.
- When you file papers or complete a task on organizing things, thank God for the time and give yourself a cheer.

Tips for Handling Files

We can also hunt for online files and documents. Simplify the process.

- Use names that identify the file to make it easy to find with the search tool.
- Keep similar papers in a folder, and label it well, like bills, home documents, insurance, etc.

- Keep the various files in a main file labeled clearly, such as home papers or tax documents.
- If you don't have time to place a new document in the correct folder, keep it on the desktop until you can move it.

Prayer

Pray Psalm 119:45. And live them.

DAY 5

Sharing Wisdom

Then my people will live in a peaceful settlement, in secure dwellings, and in undisturbed resting places. ISAIAH 32:18

From Disorganized to Mentor

My friend Sandra Felton spent twenty-three years in a messy home until a crisis forced her to admit she had a problem, and that motivated her to change. Read about her in Week 16 of Growing a Mother's Heart and how she let go of chaos.

She did more than learn to organize her home. She shared her success and ideas on getting organized. We are called to encourage one another and share from our experience.

Read Titus 2:3-5. What wisdom do you have to share with other moms?

_____

_____

How can you encourage a friend with kindness?

_____

_____

Isaiah 32:18 is part of a psalm about a glorious future. Read it. Describe your dream future.

_____

_____

_____

Read Proverbs 14:23. What is the result of hard work?

_____

_____

What are your skills and abilities with family and home-making that you can share?

_____

_____

_____

Discuss how you can buddy with a friend and help one another with homemaking skills. Write your plans.

_____

_____

_____

Read Proverbs 22:6. Why is it important to train your children to be organized?

_____

_____

_____

Read Proverbs 29:18. Vision and guidance refer to God's Word. What does this tell us happens without God's guidance?

_____

_____

_____

This passage reminds us to not lose sight of the bigger picture. God wants us to share our faith so no one will perish. However, if your stuff bogs you down, you can't easily minister to others.

The Rich Man in the Bible (Luke 18:18-23)

A rich man asked Jesus how he could have eternal life. When Jesus pointed out the commandments to follow, he replied that he had always kept them. Jesus then told him to sell his possessions, give to the poor, and then follow him. The man became sad because of his great wealth. He missed the point that only God is good, so we cannot be good enough to enter heaven. We need to follow Jesus.

What guidance has God given you for ministering to people? How will an organized home and life help you get involved in ministry?

_____

_____

Personality and Time Management

Let's look at the personalities in relation to time perspectives.

- Social interactors drop everything for fun, a text, phone call, or knock on the door. Be sure to hold off on social network and texts until work is done. Schedule time for social fun and also time to focus on work. This person is happy to be late to make a grand entrance, but needs to respect other people's time. Putting needs of others first and arriving on time allows more time to socialize.
- Powerful directors can get too focused on goals and forget to have fun or play with their children. They need to pause and give thanks and praise, as well as plan fun activities. Make play a goal too.
- Thoughtful analyzers can spend hours replaying words said to or about them. That is not productive. It's better to forgive and move on. This person can also spend too much time trying to do everything perfect but also hates to be late as she doesn't want to be noticed. Again, lower expectations. Be happy children put clothes away even if not folded well.

- Friendly supporters want peace. They prefer to relax and not rush, so they need more time and should add time to prepare and not wait for the last minute. They need incentive to overcome procrastination, which can be a promise of relaxing or treats.

Tips for Overcoming Procrastination Excuses:

- Self-doubt: list past success(es), post mottos, and give yourself pep talks.
- Self-degradation: accept compliments, and appraise your worth in God's eyes.
- Perfectionism: lower expectations and standards, and praise yourself as you work on the project.
- Defeatist attitude/Fear of failure/what others will think: look to God not people. Focus on needs you can meet, and list past successes.
- Disagreeable tasks: just do it and get it over with.
- Guilt: forgive yourself and move on.
- Hostility/anger: realize you need to forgive and let go of control, and then do the deed.
- Overwhelmed by project size and/or time commitment: break it into small pieces, focus on one part at a time, and delegate some of the work.
- Lack of skill/supplies: seek help, training, and funding
- Don't know how to start: brainstorm with someone, and ask for help.
- False sense of timing: stop guessing, and realistically evaluate the time needed for the job.

- Priority is low: schedule it, and do it.
- Boredom: set a reward for doing it and consequences for not doing it.
- Pleasure seeker: give yourself small rewards for small parts completed.
- Habitual procrastinator: tackle one task at a time and start a new habit of doing. Or, ask an accountability partner for encouragement.
- Easily distracted person: set up an area without distractions, and lock yourself in.
- Forgetfulness: write it down and post it, or set an alarm reminder.

Read Hebrews 12:11 and Proverbs 13:24. Why is it important to train our children on being organized?

_____

_____

Read Ephesians 6:4. How can you train a child without discouraging him or her?

_____

_____

Bag of Tricks to Help Children be Organized

- Teach children to be organized by first cleaning things up together. Show them how to organize items or make a bed. Then help them do it.

- After a child learns how to organize items, follow through the training by talking a child through a cleanup process, step by step. Then ask the child to tell you the steps.
- Hang a sign that reminds a child of how to clean things up, step by step. For young ones, use pictures.
- Set routines to help children stay organized such as making the bed before breakfast, putting homework and school papers in the book bag before snack or dinner, and putting away a game before taking out another.
- Praise children when they follow the routine or put away toys. This encourages them to be organized.

Mother's Prayer for Wisdom

Show me your ways, LORD, teach me your paths. Guide me in your truth and teach me, for you are God my Savior, and my hope is in you all day long. PSALM 25:4-5 NIV

WEEK 3

Support for Moms

Weeks in *Growing a Mother's Heart*
that coordinate with this week's study

Week 9: You are Significant

Week 17: Where's My Support?

Week 21: Around the Table

Week 23: Community

DAY 1

Mom Support

Look at how good and pleasing it is when families live together as one! Psalm 133:1 CEB

Amy's Story

Amy was a Christian on the brink of leaving her husband. She felt unloved and had no respect for him. She prayed and the Lord turned her to a passage on submission. She made a commitment to God that she'd submit to her husband thirty days, showing him respect and then she'd leave if nothing changed. She did everything she thought would please him from cooking his favorite meals to spending more time with him. Within a few days Amy cried tears of joy. As she changed so did her husband and he came home with flowers for her. He responded to her new attitude with love and cherishing her. It may not always work, but it is worth doing it for God, in response to showing love and respect for Christ.

Focus on Others First

Amy discovered that supporting and serving her husband brought harmony in the home. Psalm 133:1 also speaks of harmony within families. That's one of a mom's goals.

Read 1 Peter 4:10. How does God want us to use our strengths?

_____

_____

When have you chosen to serve your family? What happened?

_____

_____

How can each family member serve?

_____

_____

Read Ephesians 5:21-3, 21-24, 33. What word is repeated three times? What do you do to put your husband's needs and interests before your own?

_____

_____

Read the passage in Ephesians in a few other translations.

How and when are the words *submit* and *love* used? Also do a search for what *submit* means in the Greek. The word used is *hupotasso*. There are several different answers including "to identify with," and "be in support of." What should your attitude be?

_____

_____

Why might Ephesians 5 end with the words, "the wife must respect her husband?"

How can you respect and put your husband first?

_____

_____

For single moms, how do you keep a relationship going with those who give you support? How do you serve and respect them?

_____

_____

For single moms, do you have another single mom so you can support one another? If so, how do you maintain a balance between helping one another and maintaining your own family?

_____

_____

Couple Problem in the Bible (2 Samuel 6:15-23)

King David rejoiced and danced in the street at returning the ark to Jerusalem. His wife Michal despised him for what she considered looked like a spectacle. She mocked him when he came in to bless their home. He responded that he honored God. Michal remained childless, showing that her words and unrepenting heart toward her husband displeased the Lord. Through her words, she also criticized worship and God's choice of David to be the ruler.

Home Life

Read Proverbs 14:11 and 17:1

Discuss the contrast between the two women and the two scenarios in a home. Note that a house shows more wealth than a home in a tent. What matters more, having a huge, beautiful house, or a happy but humble home?

_____

_____

_____

_____

Outside support brings hope and strength. Women without husbands, and women who have husbands deployed, often need outside support. Support may come from extended family or friends.

Read 1 Thessalonians 5:11. How do you build your family members up? How do your family members encourage you? Do you thank your spouse for encouraging you?

_____

_____

_____

Read Hebrews 3:13. What do you need most in support for your family? How can the members of your study help one another?

_____

_____

Read Ecclesiastes 4:9-10. How is a good relationship in marriage important? What can you do to nurture your relationship with your spouse?

_____

_____

_____

My spouse and I made a commitment when we married to not tear the other one down, but to lift each other up. When we had children, we corrected our children when they disrespected our spouse. I loved hearing my husband say, "Do not talk to your mother like that. She is my wife and I love her." He always reacted with a smile when I said something similar about him.

How do you show respect for your supporters? How does this help children develop respect?

_____

_____

_____

Peace in the Home

Read Proverbs 17:14. How can you be a peacemaker in the home?

_____

_____

_____

How does anger or strife compare to letting out water? It can be a flood of tears or a stream of angry words.

_____

_____

_____

Read Romans 12:18. What steps can you take to create an atmosphere of peace?

_____

_____

_____

Creating an Atmosphere of Peace

Make your home a haven, a place where members can relax, retreat from problems, and find joy and peace.

- Praise one another.
- Listen with your ears, eyes, and hearts. Try to understand the other person's perspective.
- Be accepting of each person's unique strengths and help them overcome weaknesses.
- Set and follow through with consequences for squabbles.
- Eat together and use the time to share blessings.
- Pray together.

Spouse Check (or see what you know about those who support you).

- Do you know his favorite meal?
- Do you know his favorite snack?
- Do you know his most energetic time of day?
- Do you know and understand your spouse's personality?
- What do you say to show you respect him?
- Do you accept your spouse or try to remake him?
- How do you encourage your children to think highly of their father?
- Do you prepare his favorite foods when you know he'll have a hard day at work?
- Do you avoid gossiping about your husband?

Read John 14:27 and look up the song "Make me a Channel of Your Peace." Consider how to foster peace in the home.

Prayer

Dear Lord, thank you for giving us peace. Help me bring peace to my family, to dissolve fears and be an example of having inner peace in the midst of struggles.

DAY 2

Family Unity

Make my joy complete by being of the same mind, maintaining the same love, united in spirit, intent on one purpose. PHILIPPIANS 2:2

This day includes sections for married moms and for single moms, because unity looks different.

For Married Moms

That is why a man leaves his father and mother and is united to his wife, and they become one flesh. GENESIS 2:24

As a Coast Guard officer, Jim spent the three months at sea prior to our wedding. I finished wedding plans alone. He could only send mail when the ship sent it by helicopter. In the Artic Circle Jim saw icebergs and polar bears, but no ports. The constant white reminded him of the wedding but gave him no clue about the details.

Wedding plans included filling out a form for the band. Not being very musical and with no idea what Jim considered "our song," I quickly filled out the form and promptly forgot what I wrote.

Jim returned two weeks before the wedding. The time, filled with rehearsal, activities and having our families meet for the first time slipped by with no discussion about the reception.

When the band announced our dance as a married couple, Jim took me in his arms on the dance floor. The master of ceremonies announced the title, and laughter filled the room.

From my height of 5'4", I looked up. Puzzled, I glanced at my gown, and all around, and then asked, "Why is everyone laughing?"

Jim looked down from his tall 6'4" height, gritted his teeth, and said, "Karen, very slowly, tell me the name of *our* song."

I tried to say, "I Talk to the Trees." However, I broke out in giggles as I finally realized the visual impact of the song's title.

I often responded to comments about Jim's height by stating, "Life with Jim is always looking up! He continually shows me a new perspective. I still hunt for items at my eye level before looking at his eye level!"

Many differences are unseen. Jim was an early riser, a morning person who seldom kept his eyes open after 10 PM. I'm a night owl, and see the sunrise about once a year. I can't focus in the morning. That made it hard for us to find time to talk when we both were awake, but made caring for babies easy. I took the night shift, and Jim covered the wee hours of the morning.

Couples are partners, but also individuals, and that can cause trouble in the home and be a great help.

Reflect on Genesis 2:24. How have you become united with your spouse and your family?

_____

_____

What are your different perspectives within your marriage?

_____

_____

Read Matthew 19:4-9. What is the view of Jesus on marriage?

_____

_____

What do you do to help your marriage succeed?

_____

_____

List reasons you dated and married your spouse.

_____

_____

Keep this list handy and read it whenever you are upset or disappointed with your spouse.

Priscilla and Aquilla, the Biblical Couple

One New Testament couple stands out. They worked together and opened their home to strangers. They moved to Corinth when Claudius ordered all Jews to leave Rome. Read about them in Acts 18.

Paul found Aquilla because they shared the same career as tentmakers. Priscilla and her husband welcomed Paul into their home. Two of Paul's friends showed up, and their preaching stirred up trouble.

The couple left Corinth with Paul to sail to Syria and worked together. Later, in Ephesus. Priscilla and Aquila showed wisdom and love when they corrected Apollos, a new convert. They took him aside and corrected him quietly. That avoided embarrassing him. We don't know how the couple ended up in Ephesus, but they appeared to be content to travel and move together. They remained united and supporters of Paul's missionary work.

What helps you be united with your spouse and share goals?

_____

_____

_____

How do you jointly offer hospitality?

_____

_____

For Single Moms

When a woman marries, she does not anticipate divorce or widowhood. Yet, it happens far too often that a woman ends up raising children without a spouse, but she's not alone. God promises to be with her. She should also develop a network of support with friends and family she can count on to listen and help.

Peggy Sue, in talking about the pain of divorce, said, "I had a lot of pain and disappointment in my life. There was a Grand Canyon-size difference between what I had hoped and planned for and how my marriage turned out. The betrayal was brutal and ongoing. One of the best things I did for myself, and my children, was deal with my own issues. God led me to some beneficial personal growth opportunities. God provided wise friends who would let me vent and pray with me. I worked with a counselor and gave my children opportunity to work with good counselors. One day after several months meeting with a mentor, she said, "You can keep coming and we can keep talking about your ex, your coworkers, your neighbors, your relatives, your children, your church, and your concerns. But if you ever want to do the deep work of fixing things, we can do that." She chose to do the deep work so she would not pass the pain onto the children, and to heal wholly.

Wisdom from Single Moms

The following three women lived as single moms and share the wisdom they learned.

Wisdom from Yvonne

Yvonne Ortega, once divorced from an abusive situation, raised her only son. He entered the military service, but died from a medical problem after dental surgery.

What helped

I knew I wasn't the only one raising a child without a spouse and did not make a confidante out of my child. My child's friends were welcome in my home and ate what we ate. Nothing fancy or expensive, but a home-cooked meal together. I also determined I wouldn't talk about his father.

Support

Yvonne found support in a divorce group, single parent Sunday school group, prayer partners, reading the Bible, and praise music.

It's hard on the children, too.

Yvonne's experienced difficulties with her only child, and says, "My child turned his back on God because God didn't answer our prayers. I continued to pray around the clock for him and asked everyone I knew to pray for him. On weekends, I would fast. Fifteen years later God answered those prayers."

Wisdom from Linda

Linda Goldfarb divorced after four years of marriage, at age twenty-four, with two young children. She was raised in the church but did not have a personal relationship with God until age thirty-two. She found support by returning to church even though divorced moms were not embraced at that time. She joined the choir, read her Bible, dwelled on the Psalms and Proverbs, and learned to lean on God for support.

What helped Linda raise children without a spouse?

"Persistence. I decided I would not fail my babies even though I felt I had failed in my marriage. I believe the Holy Spirit was always speaking into me. I didn't know much about Him growing up, but once I recognized God's Spirit was *in me*, my world changed. He became my confidant when difficulties occurred."

How did Linda deal her own and her children's anger?

"When I divorced, my oldest was seven. He was confused and angry. He didn't know the whole story, and I was determined he wouldn't hear anything negative about his dad from me. One day, my son came into my bedroom and said, 'I hate you. I'm leaving!' In that moment God downloaded the phrase, 'I love you enough to allow you to hate me as long as it takes for you to know how much I love you.' I said that to my son, helped him pack, and opened the front door for him to leave. He looked up and me and said, 'I miss daddy.' I picked him up in my arms and said, 'I know you do. And I know Daddy loves you. We just can't be together.'"

She also realized God loves us enough to allow us to be angry with Him as long as it takes for us to know how much He loves us and our children.

Remarriage?

Linda remarried. She had felt burned and spurned, so she became more independent. She wasn't looking for a man when Sam entered her life. She was cautious for a time. Once they married God began to rebuild her from the inside. She says, "During this transformation in my life the closer I grew to God, Jesus, and Holy Spirit, the less weight was placed on my husband's shoulders to *make* me happy."

Wisdom from PeggySue

PeggySue's husband left her with seven children to raise and stayed at the same church but quickly remarried. All her children are grown and married now, and a few have babies. She remained single.

What helped?

Their daily family Bible study provided plenty of familiar and new topics and stories to dig into, and gave the assurance that there is a God, and He loves us. Prayer, Bible reading, and scripture memory were something they could do together, and their relationship with the Lord remains a touchpoint for them even as everyone is grown and living in different states.

Support

The church was not supportive or welcoming of single parent-led homes and they eventually left it for another. They stayed connected to church because of faith in God, though the church rejected PeggySue and her children. An older single mom came alongside as a lifesaver and sanity saver. Two other friends also walked the journey with her.

Choices made for safety and opportunities

She chose to have pets including horses (horses don't lie but provide affection) to build responsibility, gave children music lessons to develop a lifelong talent, and joined a great homeschool group for friendship. Chores also developed responsibility and nurtured her children's growth.

Single Mom Choices

How do you lean on God?

_____

_____

_____

How do you help your children cope with their emotions?

_____

_____

Where have you found support?

_____

_____

Single Mom in the Bible

The first single mom in the Bible was Hagar, unmarried and forced to have a child and then abandoned and driven into the wilderness. God heard her cry. Read Genesis 21:14-20. The name *Ishmael* (Hagar's son) means God hears.

When has God answered one of your prayers for help?

_____

_____

_____

Read 2 Kings 4:1-7. What happened when the widow, another single mom, cried out to Elisha, one of God's servants?

_____

_____

How did Elisha support her?

_____

_____

How does God's support for these two moms encourage you?

_____

_____

_____

Read Isaiah 54:5 and Hebrews 13:6. How are you a mom partnered with God?

_____

_____

_____

God's Promises

God's Word promises He'll care for us and help us in our struggles. For children of divorce abandoned by father, or deceased dads, you can start by reading the following:
Psalm 68:5, God is their heavenly father
Hebrews 4:16, mercy
Isaiah 40:29, strength
Jeremiah 29:11, prosperous plans
1 Peter 5:7, 10, care
Philippians 1:6, good work completed

Relationships Help us Thrive

In marriage, be the helpmate God called you to be and appreciate your spouse.
In singleness, find healthy support and be a support for others.

Prayer

Pray Psalm 94:18.

DAY 3

Home Hospitality and Harmony

Be hospitable to one another without complaint. 1 PETER 4:9

The boys came in from swim and track practice. Their friends followed, and the brothers introduced them. Their mom invited them into the kitchen and said she'd like their help in finishing pretzels for dinner. She showed them what to do to help and they started rolling dough, basting the pretzel shapes, and sprinkling on cheese and salt. They joked as they worked while her sons set the table and poured drinks.

As they worked, the boys mentioned her husband would be home soon, and he'd lead off the meal with a prayer. One of the young men, a regular visitor, commented that the meals were fun. He joked a lot. Mom wove in a little about how they pass the food before eating. By the time they sat, everyone was prepared to join in the customs.

Guests feel more comfortable when they feel welcomed as part of the family and they don't make embarrassing mistakes. Pretzel making provided a way to create harmony and make guests feel welcomed. They usually returned and often expressed how much they preferred the meals to eating alone with frozen meals. They prayed to always have enough food at the table and God always provided, even during a jobless time.

Read Genesis 18:1-15, 21:1-8.

What did Abraham ask Sarah to do when unexpected company arrived? What did Abraham do? How did they help one another?

_____

_____

What did Sarah do while the men talked?

_____

_____

_____

At last Sarah had a child of her own. Yet she was not content. Abraham's son by his servant was thirteen (the age of a man in those days).

Read Genesis 18:9-14. What happened, and how did Abraham try to make Sarah happy?

_____

_____

For single moms, how do you find contentment when you have so much work? How do your children help? Who else helps you release stress?

_____

_____

Read Genesis 25:9

Despite many differences, deceptions, and separation, Abraham's sons came together when he died. If you are part of a family torn by divorce, separation, or widowhood, what can you do to keep peace in the family?

_____

_____

Read Proverbs 31:10-12, 30

How can you stay focused on building a friendly home?

_____

_____

Children in the Middle

Children can be a great blessing but raising children can also cause contention. Kids tend to be selfish and want their way. They will play one parent against the other. I recall when my oldest wanted to cuddle with me in bed. My husband lay beside me, and our daughter climbed up and snuggled with her me. Before long she wiggled her way between us, and then said, "Now I feel loved."

She wanted to be in the center with both parents focused on her. That's okay some of the time, but not when children want to divide parents to get their way. Favoritism from parents also causes problems

Isaac and Rebekah and Favoritism (Genesis 25:21, 27-28)

Playing favorites and children who play up to that favoritism does not make a happy family. Isaac preferred Esau while Rebecca favored Isaac. This caused jealousy between the brothers, especially when Rebecca convinced Jacob to steal his brother's blessing and helped him do it. It took the brothers years to bridge the divide and reunite.

Read Genesis 27 and 33 to see how these choices played out in the lives of Jacob and Esau. Have you ever been a victim of favoritism?

_____

_____

_____

How can you show love to all your children and celebrate each one's uniqueness?

_____

_____

How does favoritism disrupt harmony and make the home unpleasant for guests?

_____

_____

Re-read Genesis 2:24.

Children will grow up and leave to start their own families. What can you do to keep your bonds strong within the family as children grow?

_____

_____

Read Romans 2:11 and Proverbs 15:29. Understanding God desires the best for us can be hard to grasp. Discuss God's love and impartiality for all believers.

_____

_____

_____

Read 1 Timothy 5:21. God does not want us to play favorites but that does not mean doing the same thing for each child. Boys don't always want dance lessons and girls don't always want to investigate bugs. How you show you love without complaints of favoritism?

_____

_____

Read Luke 6:31, the Golden Rule. What type of treatment does it mean? How can you apply that to guests?

_____

_____

Read Proverbs 16:3,9. It's good to make plans, especially when you commit them to God and let God guide you. This goes in marriage too. My husband Jim and I met once a month to pray together and make plans for their family and future. It made such a difference to give them a united direction and keep peace and build a hospitable atmosphere. It kept us united.

Pray and Plan with Your Spouse (or your support people)

Meet with your spouse once a month or quarter to plan and pray for your family. (Moms without spouses, remember that God is your partner, and you are not alone. Consider meeting with another single mom to have an accountability partner and build support). Start with a prayer.

- Open you calendars. Go over each person's known activity dates. Note any conflicts and discuss how to resolve them.
- Make a note of stressful times for a particular person. Circle in red the dates of anyone's hectic schedule as a reminder to pray extra for the person on those days. Consider ideas to help make the day less stressful for the busy family member.

- Pray for each family member.
- Write down the one greatest need of each person for the month and the one greatest praise. Brainstorm ideas to encourage talents and successfully overcome struggles.
- Schedule family workdays as well as fun-filled outings for the coming month.
- Discuss family relationships, needs and joys. Don't let this become a gripe session. Each spouse who brings up one desired change should also share a joy about the family. Discuss possible changes and choose one to try.
- Discuss long-term family goals, including vacations, home improvements, career goals, and educational goals. Break goals into steps. Plan to implement one step over the next month.
- Chat about parenting techniques that are effective and ones not working. Brainstorm and choose new methods, if needed.
- Discuss finances when needed and how to stay within the budget or ways to add income, if needed.
- Share scriptures that come to mind. Discuss the verses and how God may be using them to provide direction.
- Pray for the needs and praise God for the joys.
- Schedule a date for the next pray and plan, and mark it on calendars.

Prayer

Read Romans 12:16. **Pray** for harmony with guests.

DAY 4

Service

Do not merely look out for your own personal interests, but also for the interests of others. PHILIPPIANS 2:4

Selfishness

It's amazing how little children can disrupt a home with their own desires. My oldest daughter wanted control before age three. She wanted to choose where everyone sat at meals, choose what games her little brother should play, and more. Her brother naturally reacted with pushing and grabbing when she tried to control what toys he held.

We slowly taught them to share and gave our daughter control over the diaper bag and cleaning her room. She relished those tasks. She also learned to show a few toys to her brother and ask him to pick the one he wanted. As he grew, we worked on his sharing with his little brother and compromising with his older sister. He had a good sense of humor, so we used jokes and laughter to make games fun when he lost, and he realized that was better than being a sore loser.

It takes time to help children learn to share and cooperate. But it's worth it when they grow up and still get along.

Read Ephesians 3:14-21. When family is mentioned in this verse, a prayer follows it. What hopes are expressed here? How will those qualities in your family impact guests?

_____

_____

Do you ask for God's strength daily and for Christ and His love to dwell in your heart? How can such a prayer be great to say each morning?

_____

_____

Ephesians 3:20-21 remind us of God's power and ability. How might that help you rely on God's help in your marriage and family?

_____

_____

_____

Read James 4:1-3. What is the source of many problems and fights?

_____

_____

What do you do to help your children love one another and get along?

Read Genesis 33:10-15. Jacob worked at peace when he returned home. Esau accepted the peace offerings. Their mother had died. Discuss dreams for your children to get along. How does a peaceful home impact any visitors?

Children can view life differently and think there's favoritism even when you try to be fair. My oldest son accused me of being unfair because we spent more money for his sister's dance lessons than we spent on him. I offered to let him take dance also, but he balked at that. I explained that town taxes supported his sport, but we needed to pay for his sister's activity. We encouraged activities that fit each one's interests. He got it.

Read Colossians 3:14. What brings harmony?

Jesus, the Servant of All

Read each verse and then write how Jesus served people:

John 6:1-11 _____

Matthew 21:14_____

Romans 5:8_____

Read Mark 10:45. What was Jesus' attitude about serving others and putting them first?

_____

_____

Children and Service

Joseph's mother fell and sprained her ankle. He helped her in the house and offered to make dinner. His siblings set the table and cleaned up after the meal. They all continued to pitch in while mom's ankle healed. They were thankful when she was back on her feet and continued to help more. She thanked them each time and they all responded that they liked to help out.

Read Romans 12:5-7. What gifts did God give each child? How do gifts make your children unique?

_____

_____

How do you respond when your children help?

_____

_____

Read Romans 15:7. Note the key word to harmony is acceptance. Do you accept each of your children or try to make
them over to be like one another? Do you compare your
children to one another or other people's children or do
you praise each one for their own abilities and strengths?

_____

_____

When you praise your child for helping, how do they
respond? How can they show acceptance to guests?

_____

_____

_____

For single moms how do you react if outside support
appears to play favorites among your children?

_____

_____

Rejoice in each one's blessings and show by example that
you accept each child.

Harmony Tips for Parents

- Celebrate joy once a week and use the time to rejoice over each person's talents and any accomplishments.
- Praise your children when they congratulate a sibling.
- Express love to each other and your children. Understand what makes each one feel loved to fulfill their need. (*The Five Love Languages* remind us that they may want words of affirmation, gifts, service, touch, or time spent with them.)
- Have each person state one blessing and one prayer need. Let the next person pray for the need and thank God for the blessing. In praying for one another children develop compassion and more interest in encouraging one another.
- When children fight wait for them to be calm. Discuss what happened and what to do in the future. Forgive one another and pray together.

Service Opportunities for Children

- Help make sandwiches for the homeless.
- Give away clothes your kids outgrew and toys they do not need.
- Help cook and serve food.
- Clean up after meals.
- Care for pets.
- Safely pick up litter.

- Fetch things for other family members.
- Help a younger sibling or friend learn a skill.
- Help with yardwork.

Prayer

Lord, help us serve one another with love.

DAY 5

Beloved

So, as those who have been chosen of God, holy and beloved, put on a heart of compassion, kindness, humility, gentleness, and patience; Colossians 3:12

I grew up in a small town my family helped found centuries ago. As the oldest girl of my generation and the second oldest child, I felt cherished. Grandparents, aunts, and uncles doted on us. They welcomed each new child with joy and love and so did I. My younger cousins looked up to me and I loved to help them and play with them. Being beloved flows from mutual love.

I considered my dad the kindest man I knew and married an equally kind man. Both men cherished me. They listened to me, performed kind acts to make me smile, and spent time with me. I cooked what they liked, listened to them. I cared for each as they faced their last days and spent time with them.

Many women do not have such a wonderful background, but you can have a wonderful future. God already loves you and calls you beloved. Invest in loving people and serving them in a way that makes them smile. Many will return that love to make you feel loved. Those who are self-absorbed from mental illness, chronic pain, or abuse may be less capable of returning love, but they need it more and God will bless you as you bless them. I have a mentally handicapped brother and the love is more on my side, but I can tell through his smiles that kind actions make a difference to him.

You are Loved

God's love for you is extravagant and unlimited. Write about God's love next to each verse.

Psalm 149:4

_____

_____

_____

Jeremiah 31:3

_____

_____

Romans 8:38-39

_____

_____

_____

Ephesians 2:4-5

_____

_____

1 Peter 2:9

_____

_____

Beloved as Wives

Read Proverbs 31. Read Proverbs 31:10-11, 27-28. What causes a man to praise his wife and treasure her?

_____

_____

When spouses work at meeting one another's needs and put the other person first, the marriage has a stronger foundation. There are still temptations in the world. Part of the Lord's Prayer focuses on temptation. Read Luke 11:4. Why might you want this to be a daily prayer?

_____

_____

Read Philippians 4:6-7 and Proverbs 4:24-27. How can you guard your heart and not let it harden?

_____

_____

Reread Ephesians 5:31, and Hebrews 13:4. What is God's plan for marriage? Write a prayer for your marriage.

Read Song of Songs 1:1-5. Notice the passion. What do you do to keep the romance in your marriage? What do you do to retain your loveliness inside and out?

Read Esther 2:9, 12. Esther won a beauty pageant and received cosmetics and spa treatments before she saw the king. We need to nurture our beauty. What do you do to prepare yourself before your husband arrives home?

Read Esther 5:1-3. Esther had a great request to make of her husband. She didn't just go and plead with him. She dressed up, served him a favorite meal, and waited until he was ready to listen. What do you do when you want to discuss a need or desire?

Read Song of Solomon 5:10-16. The bride praises her husband and values him. She calls him her beloved and her friend. When have you praised your husband and talked to him as your closest friend?

_____

_____

Beloved as Mothers

I love how my children call me for Mother's Day and how they all came recently for my birthday. I love their concern for me when I was very ill. It's even more of a blessing that my children call me all year, that they love the Lord, and those who are parents invest so much in their children, and that they love one another. I am blessed with our great family bonds.

I also love the stories of my friends whose children celebrate them as mothers, especially those who are single moms. Single moms remember you are not alone. You are partnered with God and forever beloved. Shine for him.

However, my heart cries for friends who are moms but their children are estranged. They live with anguish as they pray for those children. God honors you as a mother and listens to your prayers and sees your tears. It does not diminish your motherhood but simply has you on a different path for now.

My heart also cries for the mothers who have lost a child on earth. You are still a mother. Be comforted that God holds your child.

Read Psalm 139:13. He chose you to be a mother and knit a baby in your womb. You were singled out for motherhood. God entrusted these lives to you because He believes in your ability. What are some of your precious mom memories?

_____

_____

Read 2 Timothy 1:5. Mothers who share their faith with their children are to be praised. Charles Spurgeon wrote, "You are as much serving God in looking after your own children, and training them up in God's fear, and minding the house, and making your household a church for God, as you would be if you had been called to lead an army to battle for the Lord of hosts."

We see through Timothy the outcome when children see a mother who lives her faith. When and how did you share your faith with your children?

_____

_____

Read Isaiah 49:15. God will never forget you as a mother or a woman. Even when your child ignores or dishonors you, God will bless you.

_____

_____

Read Luke 6:38. God reminds us that we will receive back what we give. Love your child and you will receive love. If your child turned away, then nurture another child God sends your way. How has another person returned your nurturing love?

_____

_____

_____

Read Jeremiah 31:3. God's love is everlasting. You will always be God's beloved. Thank God for His love. Look at photos of your child from over the years and recall the smiles and laughter. Thank God for those precious moments.

_____

_____

_____

One friend opened the door on her son's birthday and received a surprise bouquet of roses with a note that said, "I'm so thankful to be your son." When has a child surprised you to show his or her love?

_____

_____

_____

_____

Forever Bride Treatment

Take time to keep the glow of being a bride or a mother partnered with God. Single moms, make a habit of investing time into your inner and outer beauty.

- A few minutes to refresh your looks before your husband arrives shows you care enough to look your best for him.
- Rest, and don't over commit your time. Schedule in time to relax and refresh yourself.
- Invest a little in beauty treatments that help. There are many you can create from ingredients in the kitchen.
- Do an evening inventory of your own behavior. Did you act with love during the day? Did you hurt anyone or let your princess crown slip with not being virtuous? If so, ask for forgiveness and plan to be kinder, gentler, and more loving tomorrow.
- Remind yourself that God loves you, and you are lovely. Dress up for the Lord!

Forever a Beloved Mom

Rejoice in motherhood and be the mom your children need. They will rise up and praise you when they grow up.

- Love each child fully.
- Share your faith with your children and pray together. That's eternally important.
- Model integrity and strength.

- Take care of yourself and keep in shape.
- Act like God's princess because you are His child.

Mother's Prayer

Pray for the Lord to nurture the Fruit of the Spirit of Galatians 5:22-23 in you as a mother.

WEEK 4

Money Perspectives and Balance

DAY 1

Money Crises Before the Wedding

Make sure that your character is free from the
love of money, being content with what you have;
for He Himself has said, "I will never desert you,
nor will I ever abandon you," HEBREWS 13:5

Shortly before Rebecca's and Larry's wedding Larry, a sergeant in the Army, received news that his pay would be withheld for several months due to an error in his past pay. Normally only a portion of the pay would be withheld. Rebecca worked, but they had planned their budget on the combined incomes. They stressed over this for a few days until an officer convinced the paymaster to change to a partial withholding. They also discovered Larry had a bad credit score because a trusted family member had not understood to forward his car payments during his past deployment to Korea.

Rebecca felt shocked and betrayed. Larry realized that Rebecca had a hard time talking calmly about money problems. However, she remained calmer if they talked in the middle of a busy restaurant. Rebecca wouldn't get up and stomp out in the middle of a crowd. They could even pray over the problem in the restaurant. Thankfully, they received many wedding cards containing money and happily left on their honeymoon.

They needed to manage money as a couple. Larry liked to spend money and never learned how to save. He easily laughed, "It's only money."

Rebecca liked to save to a point of being a miser. She said, "We need to save for the future and unexpected disasters."

Their different perspectives brought lots of tension until they worked out a budget that gave them each an allowance. Larry could spend his allowance and learned that once gone he had to wait for his allowance. Rebecca saved hers up for bigger goals. They budgeted savings for a home. After five years, they bought property and qualified for a mortgage.

Spouses each need to discover how the other views money, find a healthy balance, and choose a system to budget.

Reflect on Hebrews 13:5. What is your perspective on money, spending, and saving?

_____

_____

_____

_____

How do you think your spouse views money?

_____

_____

What unexpected bills or money news have you ever received?

_____

_____

Did your spouse ever make a money decision that upset you? Why and how did you respond?

_____

_____

Who pays the bills and works up the budget? Why?

_____

_____

When, where, and how do you best discuss your family finances?

_____

_____

Biblical Money Crisis (Based on 1 Kings 17:11-16)

No rain for three years. Not a drop. Brooks and other water sources dried up. Elijah went and found the widow

God told him to visit. He asked her, "Please get me a little water in a cup."

She started to get him water when Elijah requested food. She pleaded with him since she wanted to be hospitable. "As the Lord your God lives, I have no food, only a handful of flour in the bowl and a little oil in the jar; and behold, I am gathering a few sticks so that I may go in and prepare it for me and my son, so that we may eat it and die."

Elijah told her not to fear. He shared a great secret that God chose to send her a miracle. Her flour and oil would not run out until God sent rain again. But first she needed to make him a little bread loaf and make loaves for her son and herself. She followed his instructions. Everything happened as predicted. They ate for days, and the flour and oil did not run out. God blessed this single mom and provided for her. We are never told if she even prayed for help, but she obeyed Elijah's words.

God Knows Our Needs

Read Philippians 4:15-20. What did God do for Paul?

_____

_____

What did Paul say in verse 19 that God will do?

_____

_____

What is the difference between a need and a want?

_____

_____

Anxiety over money causes stress. Read Matthew 6:25-33. What does God tell us to do instead of worry?

_____

_____

God filled the sky with birds and their sounds are often the first sounds heard in the morning. It's like waking us up with a tweet reminder not to worry. What helps lessen your anxieties?

_____

_____

Coping with Financial Anxiety

Take steps to overcome worry

- Identify the problem. Is it overspending, job loss, inflation, or emergency expenses? Be specific.
- Read and trust God's Word. Read Hebrews 13:5 that God is with you.
- Take care of yourself physically. Avoid stress eating or other unhealthy habits. Exercise and drink lots of water to be hydrated and physically well.

- List what you need and what you want but could do without.
- Eliminate any spending you can. That may be harsh if it means cutting back on fun activities and eating out.
- Create a budget.
- List other ways to make income such as selling items, downsizing, another job, working from home, getting a loan, or consulting a financial expert for help with debt reduction.
- Focus on your blessings and positive thoughts

Read 2 Corinthians 12:8-10. God tells us He is strong when we are weak. If you have been weak willed on spending, feel afraid if you lost your job, or suffered a financial loss, trust God to help you get through the struggle. How has God helped you in the past?

_____

_____

_____

Be proactive. What can you do now about the problem? Do it.

_____

_____

_____

_____

Read Psalm 150. Look to God and dwell on His power. That can help calm an anxious heart. What are your reasons to praise God?

_____

_____

Thankfully there are organizations that help people in times of need. What resources are available in your community?

_____

_____

Prayer

Pray the words of Matthew 6:33 and Philippians 4:19.

DAY 2

Unexpected Financial Woes

Consider it all joy, my brothers and sisters,
when you encounter various trials. JAMES 1:2

We didn't expect my husband Jim to lose his job, but he did, as the company moved toward bankruptcy. He had a military pension, but our first child had just started college and two more children were already in high school. Our income covered the mortgage and utilities. We also had savings but hoped we would not need to dip into that money.

We started contacting friends who might have work, went to a local job search organization, and we tightened our budget. The schools approved our applications for free lunches for the children. When the dance teacher heard we'd have to withdraw our younger daughter, she offered a scholarship. Jim offered to clean carpets for a reasonable rate, and had several offers.

He had short term jobs and part time jobs, but not full-time employment for sixteen months. God provided during that time. Jim continued to apply for jobs weekly all during that time. I had just started writing and found a few places that liked my work and paid quickly. I wrote more for them every time an unexpected expense came up, like car repairs.

We thanked God as he supplied food in unexpected ways, led us to special very reduced sales of needed items, and more. We prayed and trusted God.

What financial difficulties have you faced?

_____

_____

How did God bless you during that time?

_____

_____

Read Malachi 3:10. We tithed through the crisis. That's part of trusting God. How have you shown you trust God?

_____

_____

Unexpected Biblical Financial Woes

Job remained faithful to God. That seemed easy when he had great wealth and many children. He lost all but his wife in one day. Enemies attacked, killed some of his servants and stole his ox and donkeys. Fire rained down from heaven and destroyed his sheep and more servants. Other enemies stole his camels. A tornado struck his oldest son's home and killed him and also killed all Job's other children. Job fell ill with boils from head to toe. That's a lot to cope with at once.

God allowed Satan to cause all this damage. Job still trusted God although he questioned God. God finally reminded Job that He created everything. Job repented that he had questioned God's actions. God restored Job and his wealth and blessed him with more children.

Read Job 1:8-19. What tragedies and financial hardships did Job face in one day?

_____

_____

How have you responded to God when you have faced hardships?

_____

_____

It's hard to prepare for the unexpected, whether good like a raise or inheritance, or difficult like a broken toilet, theft, or devastating storm. Thieves, robbers, and con artists, plus identity theft and unexpected bills are just a few money disasters that happen in life. What money woes have you suffered?

_____

_____

What movies have you watched where someone tried to make a repair and caused a more expensive problem (like "The Money Pit")? How can that help you laugh at problems?

_____

_____

_____

Looking back after recovering from a money problem is much easier. Sometimes you can even laugh at that past. What money problems are now in your past?

_____

_____

Little Helper

As we planned for a move, unable to sell our home, we started building a new house in Florida. I remained in Connecticut with the children and started substitute teaching to relieve our tight finances. We shared with the children about our plans and struggles. Our youngest daughter brought me all the quarters she had saved (a few dollars) and wanted us to use them to help buy the new house so we could be together. I told her she didn't need to do that, but she insisted and reminded me, "I'm part of the family and we're all supposed to help one another. I want to help pay for the house." Children can be so astute.

Children are sensitive to our struggles. How do you share about money with your children?

_____

_____

_____

How do you talk about financial hardships or unexpected expenses as a family?

_____

_____

_____

Read Philippians 4:6 and Luke 12:25. God tells us to focus on Him and not worry about things. How do you turn off worry and trust God?

_____

_____

_____

God Provided

During another period of a tight budget, Michael drove to his youth group meeting. One night someone broke into the van and stole his backpack. The loss included a brand-new AP history book, and special calculator, and a Spanish translator. I reworked the menu and switched plans for buying a family treat to allow $35 for replacing needed items.

We prayed about the situation as a family. The next afternoon we searched the paper for sales. At one store, our youngest child pointed to a sale bin.

Michael shouted, "Mom, my same backpack is on sale and the Spanish translator is half-price. He also grabbed a graphing calculator in the sale bin. The three items stayed within the $35.

At dinner we praised God and discussed the remaining problem of his stolen textbook.

Daniel said, "God will have to get it back." Every time anyone read a book to Daniel, he prayed for God to give Michael his book.

About ten days later, I called a teen in the ministry I directed. He asked, "Did Michael throw away a schoolbook?"

"No, but he had one stolen." The thief tossed the book onto the friend's driveway, and his friend saw his name inside the book.

Read Job 42:1-6, 10-13. How did God restore Job's finances and life?

_____

_____

_____

_____

Psalm 126:1-4 reminds us that God can restore us, and our wealth. When has God provided or sent an unexpected blessing?

_____

_____

_____

Bag of Tricks for Children During a Money Crisis

When we had a tight budget as the holidays approached, I made little catalogues for each of my young children. I had three pages where they could choose one item from each page that they really wanted. I knew the grandparents would each buy one large item and that we could afford something little or make something. Only one page had the large items. They studied their little catalogues for days and finally made their choices. They enjoyed their gifts and stockings full of little surprises.

Here are some other ideas:

- Give a child a promise coin to be redeemed at a time of your choice. That will be when you have the money to give them a special gift.
- Check out free parks and activities and be sure to have outings regularly. You can have lots of free fun.
- Instead of inviting friends to a dinner at your home where you provide everything, schedule a potluck meal where everyone contributes to the food.

- Treat your children with a dollar plus tax to a dollar store to buy an item. They are sure to find something fun they will enjoy. Pick up a bottle of bubbles too and have fun with those.

Prayer

Read and pray Job 1:21.

Praise helps us focus on God, so praise God for who He is and what He does.

DAY 3

Money 'Tudes

For the love of money is a root of all sorts of evil, and some by longing for it have wandered away from the faith and pierced themselves with many griefs. 1 Timothy 6:10

I opened my high school graduation gift and looked at the locket. I smiled and held back tears. I had been saving money from babysitting for more than a year for a sewing machine to take to college. I only asked for the last of the money needed to buy it as my gift. I seldom shopped for frivolous things. My parents were well off but wanted us to have a good attitude toward money. My mother chose to give me something that would last.

I prayed for God to help me find more jobs to earn the rest of the money I needed. My father later gave me the money and told me to buy the machine. I was so thankful. I used that machine for years. I made gowns for college balls, three-piece suits for my tall and lean husband since finding them was nearly impossible, clothes for the children, and gifts. I even bartered my sewing skills with friends for services or desired items.

I still have the locket although the machine has been replaced. My parents wanted the best for me in what they chose.

Read Acts 9:36. Dorcas made clothes for the needy and friends. They praised her generosity. How do you use your talents to be generous or save money?

_____

_____

Read Psalm 37:4. God wants to bless us and give us what we desire when we commit our way to him. Instead of complaining we can continue to trust God. When have you received something you desired?

_____

_____

A Greedy Dude

A rich man decided to build new barns to hold all his grain and continue to store it. He planned to sit back and enjoy his money for years. [Luke 12:15-21].

Jesus called the man "greedy." Greedy wanted all of what he grew for himself. God called him a fool and said he would die that very night. Jesus said, "Such is the one who stores up treasure for himself and is not rich in relation to God."

Those words of Jesus implied that the man never shared from his wealth or helped people in need. He grew a crop that could have fed the hungry and still remained wealthy.

Read 2 Corinthians 9:7. Generosity makes God smile. How are you generous?

_____

_____

Read 1 Timothy 6:10-11. What is the source of evil? Why do you think this is true?

_____

_____

Have you checked your money 'tude lately? Take this quiz and see how you score.

What's Your Money Perspective?

Check off statements that reflect you.

- ❑ I'm a shopaholic.
- ❑ I believe money can improve my life.
- ❑ I deserve blessings.
- ❑ I count every penny.
- ❑ I love to buy gifts for others.
- ❑ I live in fear of not having enough money to pay my bills and try to save more.
- ❑ I focus more on relationships and living a balanced life. Money is just a tool that helps me do that.

- ❏ When I receive a gift, I judge the giver's love by how much they spend.
- ❏ I budget my money so there's enough for God, bills, savings, and fun.
- ❏ I save for things I want.
- ❏ I charge what I want and pay it off later (or try to).
- ❏ I have lots of debt.
- ❏ I have little or no debt.
- ❏ I always tithe.
- ❏ I give what I can to charity/church.
- ❏ I pay the minimum on my credit cards.
- ❏ I always pay off my credit card the month I charge anything.
- ❏ I eat out a lot.
- ❏ I cook at home and eat out for special occasions.
- ❏ Recently I needed financial help from family members.
- ❏ I worry we won't have money for repairs.
- ❏ I have money invested.
- ❏ I shop only for what I need.
- ❏ I compare prices before making a major purchase.
- ❏ I believe in spending money for training/education that will advance my career.
- ❏ We fight over money.
- ❏ We weigh pros and cons and make money decisions together peacefully.

Reflect on your answers and decide which of the following describes you best (notes in parentheses reflect extremes)

- Spender (charge when you don't have money)
- Builder (you invest money in what you think will pay off later, and may have sunk cash into scams)
- Giver (you buy gifts and pay for everyone when you eat out even if you can't afford it)
- Saver (you put money in the bank for future needs and don't want to make the purchase you saved for)

What is good about your attitude, and what do you need to change?

_____

_____

_____

What steps can you take to have a balanced view of money? For example, if you are a spender and react to stress by shopping, consider shopping at a dollar store when you feel a need to shop.

_____

_____

_____

Finding a Budget Plan

The best way to balance your attitude is to make a budget and choose how to spend and save. Choose one attitude or money habit you need to change and choose ideas to help you change.

_____

_____

_____

Read Luke 14:28 again. Jesus wisely spoke of calculating the cost before starting to build a tower. It's important to access your money before making plans to spend it. That's the reason for a budget. Do you have a budget? Is your system to manage money working?

_____

_____

Basic Budget in Three Easy Steps

If needed, create or revise your budget.

Step 1
List your income and regular necessary expenses (rent or mortgage, utilities, tithing, food, insurance).
Note: If your expenses exceed your income, you are in trouble and need to either increase your income or reduce your expenses.

Step 2
Allocate the money for tithing and then expenses. Then subtract that from your income.

Step 3

Decide how you will use the leftover money (savings, outings, clothing, fun, etc.) and stick to that plan.

Read 1 Timothy 6:10-11 again. This states that the love of money, or a greedy attitude towards it, is the source of evil. Check to see if you need an attitude adjustment. There are two main reasons for change. One is that you reach the bottom and can't continue the same way. Have you reached bottom? If so, what will you do?

_____

_____

_____

The other catalyst for change is that you have a vision of what can be, and that vision motivates you to change. The vision is always the more positive force. Write your vision.

_____

_____

_____

What is the source of problems and evil? Why do you think this is true?

_____

_____

_____

Read Philippians 4:11-13. What is the real source of contentment?

_____

_____

Read Deuteronomy 8:18. Where does your money really come from? Who is in control?

_____

_____

1 Timothy 6:17. Where is your trust for the future? Why?

_____

_____

Read 2 Corinthians 9:6. How do your money choices impact your future?

_____

_____

_____

Read Matthew 6:19-21. Why does trusting God and looking to him free you from worry and help you have a healthy attitude about money?

_____

_____

Read James 1:5. Pray over your budget and ask God to supply any needs. What are your real needs?

_____

_____

Read 1 Timothy 6:8. What should make you content?

_____

_____

List the blessings of what you have. How can being grateful for your blessings help you be content?

Prayer

Pray for God to give you wisdom regarding money. Ask Him to help with any specific needs.

DAY 4

Enterprising Moms

Whatever you do, do your work heartily, as for the Lord and not for people. Colossians 3:23

I've watched my daughters make career choices. One became a teacher and did that for several years until adopting children. She went back into the workforce when a hurricane devastated their area, and the church congregation suffered many losses. She became the lead case manager in her area for a church foundation that observed her volunteering to help people. After the crisis ended and they moved, she wanted to stay home for work and became a virtual assistant. She loves her work.

My younger daughter and her husband struggled for years. When he returned to school to pursue a new career, she had to be the breadwinner. She prayed for something that would fit with homeschooling their five children. A friend's advice led her to being a grocery shopper and that paid the bills. Doors really opened when the pandemic hit, and she could still shop. Income more than doubled and allowed them to save and move when her husband finished school and got a job offer in another state. Now she works part time to help cover unexpected expenses and extras.

Moms are very creative. They are also great sources of ideas on how to earn money from home. Sometimes moms work out of need and other times they do it to save money or provide for some extras.

What have you done to earn money, and why?

_____

_____

I have a degree in math, so money management comes easy to me. That's not true of everyone. If finances are harder for you, study any money management weaknesses online, or seek help.

_____

_____

_____

Now I am a writer and earn money from that. I started writing when my oldest started college and the youngest started preschool. I began because God called me to write. It allows me to be more generous in giving. Has God called you to do something in addition to motherhood?

_____

_____

Some people have the time and luxury to volunteer. Where and when do you volunteer?

_____

_____

An Enterprising Woman of Value

The Bible shares great praise for one woman known as the Proverbs 31 woman. She used her time very wisely both in work and homelife, plus generously help the needy. It's hard to think she did it all at the same time, and indeed it may have been a lifetime of activities.

This lady is praised by her children and husband. Merchants respect her as they trade with her. She is wise with finances and has enough to help provide for her family.

Read Proverbs 31:10-16, 20-22, 24. What are some of the ways this woman helped with family finances?

_____

_____

_____

How do you help with money?

_____

_____

_____

How do you use your talents to save or earn money?

_____

_____

Read verses 15 and 20 again. Note what she does. She may rise early, but I am not a morning person, so I stay up late. I need time to wake up and get going. We need to do what fits our own personality, schedule, tendencies, and needs. How do you make the most of your time?

_____

_____

Zucchini Bread Stand

One summer our yard overflowed with zucchini, so our children decided to set up a bread and muffin stand. We baked and packaged the bread and muffins, and they started selling it. We lived in a location where workers walked by at lunchtime. The children also sold zucchini and copies of the recipe. Every day they sold out. In a month, they accumulated quite a bit of money. They tithed it, divided it, and used some to cover the cost of ingredients. Our children learned about enterprise and made choices on what to do with their share.

We want our children to learn the value or money and have the right attitude towards it also. 2350 scriptures in the Bible mention money, so it's important.

Consider how the following verses apply to teaching children about money, treasure, and generosity:

Proverbs 29:17_____

Deuteronomy 11:13-19_____

1 Timothy 4:10-11_____

Children can help with family finances in small ways, such as saving gas by walking or biking to friends. They can cut coupons and look for coupons online, help with home repairs, and grow vegetables. How have you encouraged your children to earn or save money?

_____

_____

Children can also gather toys and clothes they no longer need to sell at a yard sale or online. Have you tried that? If so, how has it worked out?

_____

_____

Building skills equips children to be enterprising in the future. What talents have you nurtured in your children that they can use in earning or saving money?

_____

_____

Read Matthew 25:21. This is from the parable of the talents. The stewards who used their talents to generate more income received praise. What do you do to use your talents?

_____

_____

_____

Conserving resources to help care for the earth is important and usually also saves money.

List ways to encourage children to save or earn money.

_____

_____

List ways to save energy and water.

_____

_____

_____

Read Luke 16:10-12. How are you a steward with your family's money? How can your children be a steward of their money?

_____

_____

What can you do to save money such as clip and swap coupons or change the thermostat by one degree to save on energy costs?

_____

_____

Money Bag of Tricks

Many of the best things in life are free. Really! Keep a list of free and inexpensive activities. Our children even used the list as they chose activities to do once they started dating. Here are some ideas to get it started:

- Bicycling or other sport for which you own equipment
- Watching a family favorite DVD
- Taking a hike
- Cooking a meal or treat together
- Family or friend game night
- Star gazing
- Reading together

Read Colossians 3:17 and Titus 1:7.

Prayer

Pray as a family to be good stewards of money, time, and talents. Thank God for all you have.

DAY 5

Contentment, Motivation, and Goals

If any of you lacks wisdom, you should ask God,
who gives generously to all without finding fault,
and it will be given to you. JAMES 1:5 NIV

Fitting In

We prepared to leave Hawaii for my husband's next assignment in New York. The officer in charge of housing indicated we'd have a two-bedroom apartment. That would be tight with three children and not fit the rules for the number of rooms for which we qualified. Jim called and was told, "You don't have any children."

He replied, "What do I tell my wife those three little bodies with legs and arms running all over the house are then?" Oops. They rechecked and realized they had not updated his records. They gave us a tiny three bedroom. It would fit us but not all our stuff. I worried for a few days and then thought, "Maybe our stuff won't make it across the ocean and only what God thinks we need will be left.

I let go of worrying about the stuff and thanked God for a home. It changed my attitude as I realized all that stuff did not matter.

We reached our new assignment to find out we had a large place with huge rooms. We did have to go outside and down rickety two-hundred-year-old brick stairs to do laundry. All the furniture arrived safely, and we had great neighbors who brought us winter clothing their kids had outgrown for the cold days ahead. We thanked God.

Read Psalm 145:16. Are you satisfied with what God has given you, or are you always trying to get more stuff and more money?

_____

_____

_____

Read Philippians 4:8. How will dwelling on good thoughts help you be content?

_____

_____

Read 2 Corinthians 8:1-4. Attitude is key. This scripture shows a picture of poor people who are rich in joy. What is your giving attitude?

_____

_____

Little Gifts with Great Meaning

The Bible shares a few wonderful stories about people who gave what they could. One was a boy who gave his lunch. As a young boy he never thought about how a little bit could feed a crowd. Jesus used it to feed thousands of people. God can do anything! Read about it in all of the four gospels, including John 6:8-14. Another tells of a poor widow who put in a few coins in the temple offering. She gave all she had, prepared to starve instead of giving God a gift. Jesus praised the sacrifice she made. Read about it in Mark 12:41-44.

Read 2 Corinthians 9:6-8. What does God ask for in giving and generosity? What does He want your heart condition to be like?

_____

_____

Generous Hearts

Being generous is also an example for your children. At times we had our children decide where to give our charity money. We also worked at tithing our time and engaged in ministry together. We always tried to go the extra dollars in generosity. With names from an angel tree to buy jeans and other clothes, we filled the pockets with treats, money, and gift cards. It's a way to surprise the person receiving the gift.

You can add notes and valentine cards with sandwiches for the homeless. When you drop off clothes and toys for a homeless shelter you can include cards with envelopes that included stamps. When someone surprises you by dropping off a meal you can return the dish with a treat for the givers.

Read Proverbs 11:25. How does generosity refresh you?

_____

_____

Read 2 Corinthians 9:11. How is what you earn part of the blessings from God that He gives so you can be generous?

_____

_____

Read Proverbs 3:9-10. What do you give to God? How is that an investment in heaven?

_____

_____

_____

Read Proverbs 23:4-5. How does this passage help you maintain a balanced view and not be overly focused on saving money?

_____

_____

Future Goals

My husband and I set a goal to be able to pay for our children's college and grow our retirement. We invested in our children's talents in hopes of scholarships. God blessed our plans. By paying a little extra every month we paid our mortgage off early. We lived happily but did not overspend. Our children received great scholarships and our savings supplied the rest. It can be done. That type of planning comes when finances are going smoothy and a budget is working.

Read Proverbs 21:5. Do you set aside a little bit every month toward your future? If so, how do you manage that? If not, what little treats can you give up weekly to save a little money each month?

_____

_____

Read Proverbs 6:6. God's word reminds us that the ant that stores food is wise. How have you saved for the future (children's college, retirement, unexpected needs)?

_____

_____

How much is set aside for unexpected needs? How many months of bills would it cover?

_____

_____

How often do you pray and trust your finances to God?

_____

_____

_____

Read Proverbs 12:24 and 14:23. How do these verses motivate you to work?

_____

_____

_____

Read James 1:5 again. God beckons us to pray for wisdom. We did that in choosing how to help our children have the right attitude toward money.

Children and Money Choices

To help children not be tempted by commercials, we watched for a desired item that we knew would bore them or break easily. We mentioned that ads were for things they needed to try to sell because they were not good enough to simply sell. Then we let them have that as one of their gifts for a birthday or Christmas. It usually broke quickly, or they tossed it aside for something they liked better. Then we discussed the item. They agreed that they should not want something because commercials made it look good. They needed to investigate.

We often asked them to provide reasons for a purchase with both the pros and cons. Our youngest child really got into investigating the purchase of a pet and choosing the best one. He settled on a hamster. He loved and cared for his little Patchy and trained that critter. It was worth the money.

We also had them invest time in helping others by making sandwiches for the poor, adding notes to the wrappings, and by tithing money they earned. When our children were school age and teens, a major hurricane destroyed our area and hit our house badly. The three older ones volunteered at centers for people who lost their homes. Everyone, including the toddler, helped wash and fold clothes for friends who did not have electricity when our power was restored before theirs. We understood the need.

How are you teaching your children about money?

_____

_____

Sprinkle Joy into Lives

Love, joy, and peace are much more important than money. Choose to be generous in more ways than money and add joy to lives.

- Smile at everyone you meet.
- Listen to people.

- Play with children.
- Call a friend you have not spoken to in a while, just to chat.
- Enjoy a walk with family, or a friend, in a park or garden to experience God's creation.
- Send a greeting card to someone to add joy to their day.

Pray for opportunities to be generous!

WEEK 5

Hearts Filled with Lasting Treasure

Weeks in *Growing a Mother's Heart*
that coordinate with this week's study

Week 1: Treasuring the Gift of Life

Week 3: Choose Joy

Week 13: Be Your God-Created Mom Self

Week 26: Encouragement

DAY 1

Precious Hearts

Where your treasure is, there your heart will be also. Matthew 6:21

My preschool son Daniel kissed me and turned to leave with his oldest sister. I watched him wipe off the kiss and brush his chest. I thought, *Oh, he already thinks he's too old for my kisses.*

Daniel twirled around, looked up, and asked, "Do you know what I just did?"

I couldn't say what I thought, so I asked, "What did you do?"

He grinned and said, "I took your kiss and put it in my heart. If I'm sad or mad today, I can take it out, put it back on, and I'll feel better."

That so warmed my heart. It's the type of precious memory that moms treasure through the years.

God wants us to teach our children to do that with His Word. He wants our children and us to treasure His words in our hearts so they will be within us to meet our needs.

Children grow fast, and we only have eighteen years with them. We shouldn't fill their days with busyness. They need free time and outdoor time. It's also sad to watch moms texting while children play or turn on their electronic games. Some little ones even put their hands on their mother's faces and say, "Mommy, watch me."

What are some precious moments from this past week that you want to treasure in your heart?

_____

_____

Do you journal, snap photos, or do other things to capture memories?

_____

_____

COVID caused distancing between people except through technology. They realized the importance of relationships and strong bonds. What do you treasure in your relationships?

_____

_____

What and who does your child treasure?

_____

_____

How do you help your child bridge the gap of distance and time from friends and loved ones?

_____

_____

Read Luke 2:15-19. What did Mary do when shepherds came to visit?

_____

_____

Children like to save items that are meaningful. Where do you let your child store their keepsakes? Listen when they share why each item is important.

_____

_____

Treasured

God treasures you. He counts the hairs on your heads and even mothers don't do that (Matthew 10:30). He chose you, and loves you forever (Deuteronomy 7:6, Isaiah 54:10, Romans 8:39). His love is dependable (Psalm 136:26) and is poured into us (Romans 15:5). You are precious to God.

Read 1 John 4:16. Describe God's love.

_____

_____

How do you connect your children to God and celebrate faith as a family?

_____

_____

Discuss a commitment. Has your family committed themselves to God?

_____

_____

How do you show you treasure your faith and fill your child's heart with God's Word?

_____

_____

What books or devotionals does your child enjoy that develops his or her faith?

_____

_____

Encourage your child to keep and treasure items related to Bible stories or answers to prayers. What is one item you can encourage them to save today?

_____

_____

A Child's Treasured Relationship

Rebecca and I filled a care package. She raced off and returned with a teacup from her play set. She said, "Let's send this to Daddy. I miss having tea parties with him. Now we can both pretend we are together and have tea parties even when he's away on the ship."

She used that little playset daily. Sending off one cup showed how much she loved her daddy. He wrote back that he used it every day. I read that part of the letter daily and also listened to his recorded words at night. I sat in another room and listened because that made me feel his presence. Bonds can cross miles and oceans to keep little ones connected. That's one of the joys of children's imaginations. Pretending can fill the gaps of distance.

Read Matthew 18:3. What did Jesus say about being like a child?

_____

_____

_____

How do you respond to your child's playfulness or cute remarks?

_____

_____

_____

What helps you keep childlike wonder and faith within you?

_____

_____

How do you help your child bridge the gap of distance and time from friends and loved ones?

_____

_____

Have you encouraged your child to talk to Jesus?

_____

_____

Read Luke 12:34. Jesus said that where our treasure is that's where our heart is focused. What do you want your child to treasure?

_____

_____

Developing Hearts for Jesus

Ninety-four-percent of people who are committed Christians made their decision before age 18. It's extremely important to start building their faith at an early age.

- Read Christian books to your child and share about Jesus.

- Pray every day at meals, bedtime, and anytime you want to thank God or ask for help.
- Share prayer answers.
- Hold daily chats about faith. Use a devotional or read from a child's Bible.
- Share your childhood faith memories or your testimony.
- Use a family or child's devotional like *52 Weekly Devotions for Busy Families*.

Bag of Tricks to Nurture a Child's Relationships

Helping our children treasure people in their lives is important and helps build lasting bonds and develop social skills. Try these ideas:

- Practice conversations with tea parties. Boys like them too, especially with edible goodies.
- Practice answering the door and phone to greet people.
- Use online calls to connect children with family or even friends who moved away. Have some photos they can share on the screen as prompts for talking.
- Help your child create a scrapbook with pictures and notes of time spent with friends and loved ones. It might become a favorite book.

Prayer

Pray Psalm 119:105 with your children

DAY 2

Filling Children's Hearts Part One

Jesus then took the loaves, gave thanks, and distributed to those who were seated as much as they wanted. He did the same with the fish. JOHN 6:11 NIV

On cold days I baked loves of bread to be done as the older children arrived home from school or activities. I'd lift four loaves of bread out of the oven as they entered. I'd hear one of them yell, "I smell bread!"

We all gather around the table and chat while spreading butter on the steaming hot slices of a fresh baked loaf. The bread warmed their hearts and they opened-up about their day, each taking a turn sharing the ups and downs. We'd also decide where to bring one of the loaves, as a gift to a neighbor or friend. One, or all of us, would deliver the loaf.

As they grew up, my children remarked how they felt so loved when they arrived home on cold days to the scent of fresh hot bread. It filled their stomachs while the conversation filled their hearts.

What type of homemade bread do you enjoy most?

_____

_____

What helps your children open up and share what's in their hearts and on their minds?

_____

_____

Read John 6:35. What did Jesus call himself?

_____

_____

Read Matthew 6:11. What do we ask for in the Lord's prayer?

_____

_____

Hannah's Son Samuel (1 Samuel 1:16-28, 2:18-21)

Hannah longed for a child, prayed, and promised if God gave her a son she'd give him to the Lord to serve in the temple. She kept her promise and brough Samuel to the temple once she weaned him, possibly about age six. His name means *God heard.* Every year she'd make a new robe for him and visit him. Those must have been tender times, when she expressed her love with the robe that took such time to weave. Those annual reunions must have been so special for the family. Her sacrifice gave the Israelites a great prophet and spiritual leader.

Fill your children's hearts with what they need.

Let's look at an acrostic for H-E-A-R-T-S as a reminder of our children's heart needs.

H is for heritage

Read Psalm 127:3. How do you consider your children a gift from God?

_____

_____

_____

Children want to be accepted and feel they belong. What does it mean to be part of your family?

_____

_____

_____

My children loved to hear about family members past and present, especially on long car trips. Since my family settled in New England in the 1600s and my husband's family settled in the south almost that far back, we had lots of stories. They had their favorites like asking about Dan and his creativity to become a photographer to be able to climb Mount Everest, Great Uncle Carl's practical jokes, or the family farm in Georgia and their paternal great grandpa's funny sayings. It gave them a sense of identity and belonging. It also encouraged them to aim for goals, enjoy the outdoors, and want to try things family members had done.

God's Heritage

Beyond sharing family heritage, sharing Bible stories provides a rich faith heritage. Children can laugh at Balaam the donkey who talked, be inspired to brave actions with David fighting Goliath and more. This gives another sense of belonging and inspires children to follow God's call.

Heritage activities

- Share stories of family members
- Display family photos
- Display photos of relatives at your children's ages
- Talk about your child's arrival into the family
- Remind children you are happy they belong to your family.

E is for emotional experiences

Help children feel you care, understand, and approve of them whether they are happy, sad, or angry. Feelings reflect emotional experiences.

Read Romans 12:15. Why is it important to empathize with our children's laughter and tears?

_____

_____

When Rebecca came in and slammed the door, I knew she was upset. She would grumble and complain but not share her problem until I got her to laugh and relax. In contrast, Darlene would rush in and spill out all the good and bad that happened, so I could empathize. Michael came in, got a snack, and then shared one thing that happened. Then he clammed up.

One child may be extroverted and share easily while others are introverted and keep things inside. Figure out the best ways to interact with each child that helps them open up. Fill their life with positive emotional experiences.

Emotional Filling ideas

- Share jokes and funny family stories.
- Cry together over a sad movie.
- Hug your child when he cries and listen to what's in his heart.
- Enjoy emotional adventures together or going to the theatre, viewing sunsets, strolling through a park, and enjoying thrilling amusement parks.
- Make faces to see if people can guess the emotion shown and discuss different emotions.

A is for Affection and Affirmation

Affection shows children that they are loved and cherished.

Read Matthew 3:17. Notice how God declared his love for his son Jesus. He opened the heavens to affirm his son.

_____

_____

When we have worked hard and reached a goal, we want our family to rejoice and approve us. Children need that too. We affirm them with words, smiles, looks, and more. They want to know they are loved and that is done with words, hugs, making their favorite treats, and little actions that show you care.

Affirm Your Children

- Pass out a treat for no reason except to say, "I love you"
- Tuck your child in bed at night with a prayer and a kiss
- Lay hands and your child's head and bless him or her
- Have a family group hug
- Hold hands when you take a walk
- Let your child cuddle up or sit on your lap

Pray

Thank God for your children since they are your heritage, a gift from God (Psalm 127:3)

DAY 3

Filling Children's Hearts, Part Two

Godliness actually is a means of great gain when accompanied by contentment. 1 Timothy 6:6

Relationships and Restitution

Michael may have said he was sorry but his angry tone in his words by followed by sticking out his tongue proclaimed a different message. We want children to understand forgiveness and love one another, but that can be hard when they squabble. One leading reason children fight is to get a parent's attention.

I changed things up once. I said, Michael, you hurt your sister's leg. She has to sit, and you'll have to be her feet for a while. She was supposed to sweep the floor, so here's the broom. If she needs anything you'll have to get it for her." He noticed she had tears as he carried a drink, book, and other things to her.

It didn't take long for my son to cry out, "I'm really sorry I did that. Being her feet is not fun."

Then we discussed loving one another.

Read John 15:12. Why is it important to teach children to love one another?

_____

_____

Read John 15:11. When have you seen your children's joy spill over and cause others to smile or laugh?

_____

_____

Read Psalm 133:1. Discuss how happy your home is when everyone gets along.

_____

_____

What do you do when children fight or argue?

_____

_____

_____

How can you help children choose joy and get along?

_____

_____

R is for Robust Relationships

It takes time to build and keep relationships going strong. To a child T-I-M-E spells love. Investing time shows that the person matters and is important. We show we appreciate our child when we want to be with him or her. What do you do to build a good relationship with your children?

Because my husband loved popcorn and sitting together to talk or watch a show, the whole family loves popcorn. We pop it on the stove, shake on salt, and drizzle it with butter. It's a simple way to gather and relax. It's easy and takes little preparation.

We also liked being in the water whether swimming, canoeing, or doing water aerobics. Common pleasures help build lasting bonds. What do you enjoy as a family?

_____

_____

How can you keep conversation open as your children grow? How can you be real or authentic?

_____

_____

Bible Brothers

Two pairs of brothers served as disciples to Jesus. Andrew met Jesus first and quickly enlisted his brother. Jesus called John and James as they worked together. Both sets of brothers apparently had strong sibling relationships. Andrew and Peter shared a home (Mark 1:29). Together James and John asked Jesus a favor. Apparently, no brother minded when Jesus called more on Peter and John for the ministry work. They all followed God's call. Peter and John wrote epistles. James was the first martyr. Andrew hung on an x shaped cross, tied, and it's believed in the days while he hung he continued to preach about Jesus. They depict good brotherly relationships where they focused on Christ.

Relationship Boosters

- Be in the moment with your children. Listen to them and engage with them instead of your phone or tasks.
- Plan family outings and cleanup times to play and work together.
- When you and your spouse have financial difficulties or problems, let your children know in simple terms that grownups have problems too.
- Invest time with your children. If you travel, connect online or via phone.
- Get involved in a church ministry or activities together, where you all can be involved.

T is for Team Spirit

We cheer one another on and have always done that from celebrating a child's first step, getting a good grade, to graduations and birthdays. Most days have many reasons to be happy when you are part of your family, and opportunities to let children feel that on a team.

Teamwork extends to helping with the work of caring for the home. We raked leaves planted seeds, cleaned the house, and performed other chores together. The work goes faster, and we can all rejoice in the completed task. Even in the dailiness of meals we share in the cooking, setting the table, and clean up. Family routines help build team spirit.

Read Acts 10:2. Discuss what unity looked like in the home of Cornelius. How is it in your family?

_____

_____

Read Acts 4:32. How did the early family of believers build unity?

_____

_____

Read Ephesians 4:3. Unity takes effort. How do coaches on a good team keep players united and how can those methods help your family?

_____

_____

On a team players support one another and share a common goal. Everyone does their part to ensure success.

_____

_____

_____

Team Spirit Boosters

- Pray together.
- Help one another with chores, especially meals.
- Enlist children's help with laundry and cooking.
- Develop a family cheer.
- Cheer for one another before tests and after successes.

Read 1 John 4:16-19 and John 3:36. When have you talked to your children about God's love, Jesus, and heaven?

_____

_____

S is for Spiritual Connections

Our children grew up with family devotions and probably don't recall childhood without them. We mixed in games and hands on activities with reading the Bible. We also prayed before leaving home, at meals, and other times. That's part of building a spiritual heritage.

A faith connection gives your child assurance of eternal safety. A child's brain is most elastic for learning during the preschool years.

With that fact in mind why is it important to start sharing faith with children at a young age? How have you shared faith with young children?

_____

_____

Read Deuteronomy 6:4-8. How are you weaving faith into daily life with your children now?

_____

_____

Spiritual Filling Ideas

- Pray together at meals, bedtime, emergencies, and celebrations.
- Have a praise party to honor God.
- Read a Bible verse together daily.
- Share how scriptures have helped you.
- Act out favorite Bible stories

Read 1 John 4:7. What should be your source of love?

_____

_____

Several families I know have parents who work odd shifts. It's harder to have certain routines. They make a point of going out for a big breakfast every week or so when everyone is available. That's also the time the dad asks what they learned about God and asks about their most recent Sunday school class or church sermon. Then he asks how they put that into action. It's great to have family chats around the table that bring in faith.

Faith Chat Prompts

Consider your children's ages and interests and how to connect that with faith talks.

- Ask how a hero in the Bible made a good choice and what happened.
- Ask how someone in the Bible made a bad choice and what happened.
- Chat about the meaning of words read.
- Discuss miracles in the Bible and ones you know happened to people you've met.
- Chat about a talk or a Bible lesson at church.
- Share prayers answers. Rejoice over answers and sympathize over unanswered prayers.

Praise God for listening to your prayers

DAY 4

Personalities, Part One

*My frame was not hidden from You when I was
being formed in secret [and] intricately and
curiously wrought [as if embroidered with various
colors] in the depths of the earth [a region of
darkness and mystery].* PSALM 139:15 AMP

God creates each individual's personality or temperament.
I noticed the differences in my children while they moved
inside me. Rebecca wanted control. If I sat too long, she
started kicking and punching. Every night she had to do
her routine of twenty laps around the pool.

Michael leaped to voices. If I headed out and down the
three flights of stairs of the apartment, he joyfully kicked
so hard I feared I would fall. He kicked me off sofas and
chairs.

James seemed more sensitive to my needs. He would
tap lightly before he kicked and never kicked too hard. If
he moved much, I could rub my belly and he'd quiet down.

Darlene often remained quiet, but seemed to dance to
music.

Daniel was more relaxed. He could not bother to kick hard and mainly rolled. He seemed to enjoy just laying around inside me.

Read Psalm 139. What phrases and verses stand out? What is stated about the creation of each individual?

_____

_____

Read Psalm 139:2. How well does God know each person? How does it help to know and understand each child?

_____

_____

Read Proverbs 2:2. How will understanding your child's personality help you parent better?

_____

_____

Let's go into personalities a little more to understand how to meet our children's needs. We'll study two of the four main temperaments of personalities today and use three descriptive phrases for each type.

Social Interactor, Socializer or Popular Sanguine

Each of the personalities can be found in the Bible. Study Peter: Matthew 14:28-133, Luke 22:54-62, 24:12, Acts 2:14,

John 13:8-9, and Matthew 26:69-75. Describe Peter's character traits and behavior.

_____

_____

Peter, a talkative extrovert was impulsive, spontaneous, loud, optimistic, emotional, and joyful. He answered fast, jumped out of the boat into the water, and wanted acceptance. He liked attention.

My son Michael has that enthusiasm and zest for life. Even when nurses tried to bring down his high fever with a cool bath, he laughingly splashed them all. He could turn any punishment into fun that everyone else clamored to do.

If you have a popular socializer, what are your joys and frustrations?

_____

_____

Read John 1:42, Matthew 16:18, 23; and Luke 22:31-34. Jesus responded to Peter by giving him attention and approval to meet his personality needs. He rebuked him loudly when needed, used his natural leadership ability, and told Peter he would deny Him, but then become stronger. How did Jesus refine Peter's character?

_____

_____

Powerful Director or Mobilizer or Choleric

Study Paul. Read Acts 9:22, Acts 21:13, 1 Corinthians 15:9-11, and Galatians 2:11. What words describe Paul?

_____

_____

_____

Paul, a powerful director, or mobilizer, liked to teach and be in control and get things done. He was willing to debate to persuade people of the truth. His great passion kept him focused, but tended to make him authoritative.

Strong-willed Paul needed a hard knock of being struck by lightning. Once he chose to follow Jesus, he willingly spent three years learning. God directed Paul through the Spirit.

_____

_____

_____

My daughter Rebecca, a born teacher played school for years, tried to get her younger siblings to obey. She craved control, so I put her in charge of the diaper bag. She kept it filled with everything I needed and by the front door. If I'd asked Michael to take care of the diaper bag, it might have gone anywhere and held toys, but probably no diapers. If

you have a powerful director/mobilizer what are your joys
and frustrations?

_____

_____

Read Acts 9:4-6, Acts 16:6-7, 2 Corinthians 12:7 and Galatians 1:13-18. How did Jesus respond to Paul?

_____

_____

Read and pray Proverbs 2:2
*Make your ear attentive to wisdom; incline your heart to
understanding.*

DAY 5

Personalities, Part Two

Trust in the Lord with all your heart and do not lean on your own understanding. Proverbs 3:5

Analytical Thinker, Organizer, or Perfect Melancholy

Daniel would come downstairs after everyone else left. I usually asked how he was doing, and he'd reply, "I'm okay. I haven't seen any people yet." He liked to be alone and never wanted to be in front of a crowd. He never liked trouble. A simple scolding provided enough incentive for good behavior. He liked lining up his little cars in the same order and slowly moving them around.

Moses also liked being alone and shrunk from talking and being noticed. He probably enjoyed being a shepherd for forty years, caring for sheep and counting them. That's their temperament or personality. This one of two more types we will study.

Read 1 Kings 3:9. God told Solomon to ask for anything. What did Solomon request and why?

_____

_____

Read I Kings 3:11-12. How did God respond?

_____

Read Psalm 139:4 and John 10:14. How well does God know us?

_____

_____

Study Moses who was could be called a thoughtful analyzer, organizer, or perfect melancholy. Read Exodus 2:14-15, 3:11-14, 4:10; and Numbers 12:3. What words describe him? How did God deal with his personality?

_____

_____

Read Numbers 14:12-20 and Exodus 18:17-26. How does that show Moses was a deep thinker and analytical as well as an organizer?

_____

_____

If you have a quiet introverted analytical thinker what are your joys and frustrations?

_____

_____

Friendly Supporter, Stabilizer, or Phlegmatic

James, my phlegmatic son, could sit for hours to watch turtles or the night sky. When asked, "What do the turtles do?" He responded, "Sometimes they move." He liked to sit peacefully and think, enjoyed eating slowly, and avoided fighting with his brothers and sisters. He never rushed, liked to have lots of free time to think, and had a great sense of humor. He worked at making peace with others although he could procrastinate a lot.

Abraham avoided confrontations, sought peace, and thrived living in a desert.

Study the phlegmatic. Read Genesis 13:7-9, 18:23-33, 21:8; and Hebrews 11:17-19. What words describe Abraham?

_____

_____

If you have a phlegmatic child, what are your joys and frustrations?

_____

_____

Each personality has their own set of needs and those are clues to understanding effective discipline and motivation for them. What are we urged to do always?

_____

_____

All Personalities

All personalities have strengths and weaknesses, and God uses all types of people. Jesus reacted to people according to their personalities. God loves us all and all personalities are loveable, especially when we appreciate the strengths. The weaknesses such as the procrastination of a friendly supporter or the bossiness of a powerful director can cause problems in a relationship unless we understand the person's motivations and needs.

God worked with all personalities:

- Jesus strongly rebuked the impulsive outgoing Peter.
- God patiently responded to introverted Moses and doubting Thomas.
- Jesus zapped Paul plus gave him new goals.
- God spoke with Abraham and gave him time to be ready for his call.
- Jesus asked John his loyal and beloved friend to care for his mother.

Understanding what motivates, depresses, or supports a person's personality helps a mom know how to bring out the best and help a child overcome weaknesses.

Study the chart on the next page; List each child's strengths, weaknesses, and needs.

_____

_____

_____

Pray

Mother's Prayer. Substitute your child's name for *me*.

Search [child's name] [thoroughly], O God, and know [child's name] heart! Try [child's name] and know [child's name] thoughts! And see if there is any wicked or hurtful way in [child's name], and lead [child's name] in the way everlasting. PSALM 139:23-24

We can have more peaceful homes through understanding our children. Here's a little summary of needs in addition to others covered already.

Type	Social Interactor (Peter)	Powerful Director (Paul)	Thoughtful Analyzer (Moses)	Friendly Supporter (Abraham)
Description	Talkative, energetic, popular, loud, friendly	Natural leader, goal oriented, organizer, confident	Sensitive, perfectionist, considerate, good listener	Easy going, witty, diplomatic, peace maker
Strengths	Creative, cheerful, optimistic, enthusiastic	Ability to take charge, lead, teach	Organization, analytical ability	Balance, ability to make peace
Weaknesses	Doesn't listen well, doesn't follow through or complete tasks, manipulative	Bossy, insensitive, controling	Slow to forgive, sensitive, afraid of failure	Procrastinates, indecisive, not enthusiastic
Needs	Attention, affection, audience	Affirmation, purpose	Assurance, organization, understanding	Acceptance, respect
Leadership strengths	Inspires followers	Knows what works, sets goal	Sensitive to others, organized	Diplomatic, calm, inspires loyalty
When upset	Noisy, disruptive	Bossy, temper tantrum	Whines, cries, withdraws	Sleeps, sarcastic

(continued)

Type	Social Interactor (Peter)	Powerful Director (Paul)	Thoughtful Analyzer (Moses)	Friendly Supporter (Abraham)
Needs to work on	Listening, time management skills	Saying thanks, accepting others, sharing responsibility	Lowering perfectionist standards, accepting constructive criticism	Set goals, Overcome procrastination
Value them for	Creative ideas, enthusiasm, cheering up others	Quickness, work ethic, goal setting	Sense of detail, organization, loyalty, follow-through	Problem solving ability, peace-making ability
Gets along with	Analytical thinkers and friendly supporters who give them attention	Analytical thinkers and friendly supporters who follow them	Friendly supporters, Powerful directors who express appreciation or guide them	Analytical thinkers and those who respect and accept them
Trouble getting along with	Bossy powerful directors	Social interactors who disrupt and talk too much	Overwhelming social interactors, powerful directors	Pushy, bossy powerful directors

GROWING A MOTHER'S HEART BIBLE STUDY

WEEK 6

Making Your Home
a Haven

Weeks in *Growing a Mother's Heart*
that coordinate with this week's study

Week 16: Creating a Haven

Week 19: Faithful Moms

DAY 1

Happy Feet

*Don't forget to show hospitality to strangers,
for in doing so, some have entertained angels
without knowing it.* HEBREWS 13:2 CEB

"Will Daddy be home soon?"

"No, dear. Not until Christmas.

"My birthday comes before Christmas. Will Daddy come for my birthday?"

"Grandma and Papa will come for your birthday. Daddy will be at sea."

The questions had just begun, worse than a car trip full of the repeated pleas, "Are we there yet?"

To pass the days until Jim's return, I set up a small tree and helped Becky and Michael make an ornament daily to decorate the boughs. I said Daddy would return by the time they filled the tree. I designed a new creation during naptime and chose a Bible verse to match. Craft time became our daily devotion time. They enjoyed creativity and chatting about Christmas.

One day Becky invited a friend stating, "Amy's daddy is at sea too, so she wants to make an ornament to surprise him."

Within a week, laughter filled the house as a group of children arrived daily to make ornaments. We lived in military housing where many children waited for a parent's return from deployment.

Soon, a few mothers joined, and we'd follow art time with snacks. I talked with the moms as the children played.

When Jim returned home, he laughed as Becky described each decoration, telling how she made each one. Michael danced around the tree and pointed to ones he helped make.

She also said, "Our home filled with happy feet every day. My friends came and made ornaments. I know we like to be hospitable. Mommy told us all about Jesus and Christmas. That made it fun even though I missed you."

———————

How do you encourage your child's hospitable spirit?

_____

_____

_____

How does your family make visitors feel welcome?

_____

_____

Read Acts 12:12. How many people gathered in this woman's home and what did they do?

_____

_____

_____

How does your family share about Jesus in your home?

_____

_____

Have you ever held a children's faith-related study in your home? If so, what did you do?

_____

_____

_____

Unexpected Company (Luke 19:1-9)

Short Zacchaeus climbed a tree to see Jesus, and that changed his life. Jesus stood under the tree, called Zacchaeus to come down, and invited himself to the tax collector's home. People grumbled that Jesus wanted to visit a sinner, a tax collector. But Zacchaeus rejoiced and the visit changed his actions.

Sometimes company is unexpected, and the guests may even invite themselves over. Read Luke 19:1-9. How did

Jesus end up visiting Zacchaeus? How did that change the tax collector?

_____

_____

_____

Read Matthew 19:13-15. How did Jesus show hospitality when children came to see him?

_____

_____

We lived on Oahu in tropical Hawaii, surrounded by water. We saw the beauty of the ocean and the splendor of many waterfalls. One day it poured for hours. The streets flooded, and from our house on a hill, we watched a small pond form at the base of the driveway. Becky's excitement bubbled over. She spoke of getting ducks, a boat, and the joy of living in a lake. I worried about how Jim would get home. He phoned that he planned to bring a friend for dinner. The water left him undaunted.

I quickly surveyed the contents of a nearly empty freezer and cupboards. The only supplies on hand consisted of rice, shrimp, and pea pods. The pouring rain nixed any thought of shopping. I spent the afternoon praying that our guest was not allergic to shrimp. When I set the food on the table our guest exclaimed that he had been dreaming of shrimp and pea pods all afternoon! Rebecca announced we prayed he'd like the food.

Do you keep extra snacks or easy-to-prepare food on hand for unexpected company?

_____

_____

Do you pray for your guests and menu?

_____

_____

Read Romans 12:13. Read the verse in NLT. How do you practice hospitality and help your children learn to be hospitable?

_____

_____

Read about Mary and Marth in Luke 10:38-42. How did each woman show hospitality? What can you do to not be distracted when guests arrive?

_____

_____

Read Luke 24:13-32. How did the men react to a stranger walking up and asking what they were discussing? How did they extend hospitality at the end of the day?

_____

_____

How do hugs and waving goodbye extend the hospitality?

_____

_____

Read the following scriptures and write what you noticed about hospitality.

- Matthew 8:14-15_____
- 2 Samuel 9:1-13 _____
- Acts 16:15 _____
- Acts 28:2 _____

Safety and Strangers

We need to balance safety and hospitality. How do you show you get to know someone before extending an invitation?

_____

_____

What do you teach your children about safety and strangers?

_____

_____

Company After Bed Bugs

Mary Beth struggled after they rid the home of bed bugs. No one wanted to visit them She understood, but her family missed all the company dropping in. She chose to hold an open-house friendship party. She and her children sent out invitations, her husband cooked special treats, and they cleaned the home again. People came, and her house again became a safe place where friends dropped in.

With COVID, we are more aware of keeping our families safe from germs. What do you do to keep your family safe?

_____

_____

Read Hebrews 13:2 again and Matthew 25:37-40. Pray for your guests. Discuss how we might entertain angels when we treat guests well.

_____

_____

Bag of Tricks to Teach Children Hospitality

- Children love to pretend. Play with them. Be a guest as part of the play. They can take your coat, invite you to sit, offer you a drink, and say thanks when you leave.
- Make up picture cards to remind younger children how to be hospitable.
- Have play tea parties to help children learn to serve people and converse.
- Model manners and praise children when they say 'please' and 'thanks.'

- Enlist children to help prepare for guests with setting the table, cooking, and serving.
- Pray for guests before they arrive and after they leave.
- Clean up before guests come.
- Let your guest go first in games.

Prayer

Read Luke 14:13-14.

Pray for your heart to be welcoming to children who cannot repay your hospitality.

DAY 2

Open Door Policies

*Now in the same way in exchange—I am
speaking as to children —open wide your
hearts to us, you as well.* 2 CORINTHIANS 6:13

Hungry Knockers

One of my children's friends rang the bell often to play
at our home. One day he showed up when I was the only
one home. He asked if he could stay and promised to just
sit quietly. With some prodding I discovered an older sibling sometimes hit him. His older brother came by and
asked if he could please have a piece of bread. I asked if
his parents were too busy working to shop. He explained
they had both lost their jobs. I gave him a loaf of bread
and some other food. I also warned him that if he hurt his
brother again, I would tell my friend, his aunt. In some
situations, you may need to report abuse, but meanwhile,
let your home can be a haven of safety.

Read Philippians 2:4. This verse is a reminder to look out for others. How can you have an open heart to help others when you open your door to visitors?

_____

_____

Come to My Home!

One woman urged Elisha to eat at her home. Well, that food must have been scrumptious, for he started stopping by to eat regularly. His company never wore out the welcome mat. In fact, she suggested to her husband that they build a room for Elisha to stay when he came. Then he started spending nights there. She also realized Elisha served God and called him a holy man of God.

Read the story in 2 Kings 4:8-11. Elisha accepted the invitation one time and then made a habit to drop in anytime he visited the area. Does someone like to drop in or may have become a fixture in your home?

_____

_____

How did this woman react to Elisha coming frequently? What have you noticed about frequent guests?

_____

_____

What did the woman recognize about Elisha?

_____

_____

Read 2 Kings 4:12-17. Elisha blessed the Shunammite with a newborn son for her kindness. When have you received a blessing for being hospitable?

_____

_____

Some might call Elisha's visits divine appointments. How do you distinguish between divine appointments, interruptions, and disruptions?

_____

_____

Welcome to Our Table!

My maternal grandparents owned a large piece of property a few towns away from their house. On Sunday afternoons, after church, from spring through fall, they opened it up to family and friends. We might have one hundred people there. Everyone welcomed new visitors and people who only came a few times each year. It was a potluck, but my grandpa also brought hot dogs, burgers, and buns from his restaurant every week. It didn't matter if someone contributed food or not. From the sandbox and toys for the tots to the horseshoe court and other games for various ages, my grandparents had designed the place for fun and relaxation and to provide a free place to gather. Lots of chairs and hammocks allowed for rest, while a small pond for swimming, and a mountain offered exercise opportunities.

The hospitality shown guests taught us all to be welcoming. Everyone could return and bring their own friends. If any kids started to fight an adult would remind them to be kind. Once I married and moved away, I followed their example with inviting people to our home. Whether serving thirty-four for dinner, or just one friend, I try to share their spirit of welcoming and trust there will be enough food.

If you have planned a potluck, what makes it work well?

_____

_____

_____

Read 2 Kings 4:42-44. What happened when Elisha needed to feed a crowd?

_____

_____

A Child's Invitation

At five years old my son James asked me if he could invite his friend Stephanie for a special Christmas tea for two.

I agreed and we made gingerbread cookies and some punch. He set up the children's china tea set on our Oriental tea table. His friend arrived with her mother. James greeted her at the door, took her coat, escorted her to a seat, and served her. He imitated many things he observed his father do. They exchanged little Christmas gifts. They chatted happily. At the end he thanked her for coming. His mom said, "I want him!"

How have you encouraged your children to care for their guests?

_____

_____

Read Acts 16:40. Lydia opened her home to Paul and other followers. How is your home a place for people to visit?

_____

_____

Balance

Read Proverbs 31:27. A wise woman looks well to the needs of her home and family. She doesn't waste time. How do you balance your time with dividing it between work and engaging with guests?

_____

_____

Read Mark 6:31-32. Jesus retreated and set a boundary for rest and quiet. Do you schedule time to relax with your family?

Read 1 Corinthians 6:12. Some activities may include too much company that disrupts your home. How do you set boundaries?

Read Exodus 18:8-27. Notice what Jethro said to Moses in verses 17-18. How do you prevent being overwhelmed with too many people leaning on you?

Open Doors with Boundaries

Consider these ideas about unexpected changes in plans.

- Disruptions break into a person's time with chaos and selfish cries for attention. It usually brings noise.
- Interruptions break into another person's action for a purpose, often for an emergency or important need.

- Divine appointments are meetings or changes in plans that God orchestrates.

When to Say Yes And when to say No

- Always pray when anyone disturbs you.
- For disruptions, respond by setting limits. Let the person know your available times.
- For interruptions, assess the urgency of the situation and decide how fast to respond. If it can wait, schedule a time to handle it.
- For divine appointments, say, yes. Follow God's leading.

Read Luke 7:37-44. How did Jesus praise the sinful woman's hospitality?

_____

_____

When and how do you praise your children for showing hospitality?

_____

_____

Snack Ideas for Unexpected Company

- When making cookies, freeze some of the dough into a tube shape. Then when unexpected company arrives slice and bake the dough.

- Keep some crackers and toppings on hand (cheese spread in a jar, jams, peanut butter).

Shrimp Dip (or use canned chicken or tuna)

2 cans tiny shrimp, drained
2 8-ounce packages of cream cheese
1 8-ounce container of sour cream
Worcestershire sauce or steak sauce
Crackers, chips, or cut veggies to use with dip

1. Soften cream cheese in microwave safe dish until soft (1-2 minutes depending on microwave wattage).
2. Mix cream cheese and sour cream. Mix in a tablespoon or two of Worcestershire sauce and stir in drained shrimp.
3. Bake at 325°F for 20-30 minutes until the edges brown and the mixture starts to bubble. Serve with cut veggies, chips, or crackers.

Prayer

Pray this verse as a family to remember to be hospitable

A new commandment I give to you, that you love one another, even as I have loved you, that you also love one another. JOHN 13:34

DAY 3

Guarding Hearts and Homes

Watch over your heart with all diligence, for from it flow the springs of life. PROVERBS 4:23

Sweet Reminders

One of my sons had a friend who used bad language. Each time he arrived I offered him a mint and said, "Here's something sweet for your mouth. In our home we only use sweet words. Bad language and words that hurt are not allowed." It only took a few times of sending him home for him to choose better words.

Read Proverbs 4:23. What does this say about the heart?

_____

_____

_____

_____

Read Luke 11:21. What gives you safety in your home and protection from thieves?

_____

_____

Read Psalm 121:8. God promises to guard us as we come and go. Do you pray for God's protection before leaving home?

_____

_____

It's hard to be with your children everywhere they go. We need to trust God and make wise decisions. What do you do to guard your children's hearts?

_____

_____

King David

God chose David to be king when he was young. The youngest child in the family, David served as a shepherd where he played a lyre and praised and trusted God. He made mistakes and sinned but then asked God to forgive him. He trusted God to give him the courage to face the giant Goliath and won. Psalms David wrote, such as Psalm 23 resonate with trust and praise for God, the joy of forgiveness and desire to be holy.

David committed the great sins of adultery and plotted the murder of Uriah the Hittite, a faithful warrior. When confronted with the sin David repented. He showed compassion when he asked Mephibosheth, the son of his dear friend Jonathon, to come to the palace and eat at his table daily. Kings generally had all the family of the former king killed, but instead David restored all Jonathon's land to Mephibosheth.

Read 1 Samuel 16:7. What is your heart condition today?

_____

_____

_____

Read Psalm 24:4-5. What does it say those after God's own heart will do? How are you doing that?

_____

_____

_____

Read Proverbs 4:23. How do your emotions impact your words and actions?

_____

_____

_____

Guard Your Heart in Four Ways

1. Choose words wisely. Read Ephesians 4:29. What helps you be careful with your words?

_____

_____

2. Focus on God. Read Psalm 19:14 and Psalm 51:10. How can one of these scriptures repeated every morning help you stay focused on God and guard your heart?

_____

_____

3. Show love in action. Read Colossians 3:23 and James 1:22. How can you show your love for God through your actions?

_____

_____

4. Avoid temptation. Read Isaiah 30:21. In reading the Bible and praying, when has God guided you to make the right choice?

_____

_____

_____

How does praying the Lord's Prayer help you avoid temptation?

_____

_____

It's Just a Little Bit!

Some unusual brownies can be good food for thought. One mom called her children in for brownies and said, "I made these brownies for you. They contain just a little bit of dog poop."

"Oh! Gross, " Kids responded.

The mom said, "I would not eat them either. If we want something to remain pure and good, we need to make sure we only use good things. That includes making sure we only let good things into our hearts and good words into our minds."

The kids asked, "What about books and movies with just a few bad words or thoughts?" That launched a discussion.

Read Psalm 51:10 again. Why is it important to have a clean or pure heart yourself?

_____

_____

_____

Read Proverbs 22:11. What are you teaching your children about purity?

_____

_____

_____

Read 2 Corinthians 6:6. What helps you keep your heart pure? How are living what you teach about purity?

_____

_____

_____

Speak with Love

My friend Pam Farrell grew up in a home with lots of discord. She chose to be joyful and loving. When she found herself yelling at her children and one pulled at her clothes and said, "You're scaring me," she stopped. She repented and gathered her children to ask for their forgiveness. She whispered and said she'd remember to use her soft voice.

We need to be willing to pause and change whenever we find ourselves letting our hearts' guard down. If we fill our minds and hearts with positive thoughts and look for opportunities to praise our loved ones, we will speak more lovingly. If we catch people doing something kind, we can become encouragers.

When have you caught yourself doing or saying something hurtful or wrong? How did you react?

_____

_____

_____

Read 1 Corinthians 13:4-7. How do you measure up in loving others from your heart? What can you do to be more loving?

_____

_____

Read 1 Peter 3:8 and Philippians 4-6-8. How can these ideas help you fill your mind and heart with love and help you be an encourager more than a critic?

_____

_____

_____

List each family member and write one thing you love about the person and one thing they did lately that blessed you. Be sure to thank the person and encourage them for those and other reasons.

_____

_____

Safeguards

- Make your doorway a prayer way to pray before leaving and praise God when returning.
- Add notes into your phone of where your child will be with contact information and address.
- Teach your child to know address, phone, emergency contacts.
- Get to know the parents of your children's friends.
- Use safeguards to protect hearts with television and electronic devices.
- Read books together and continue that as your children grow.
- Keep a list of free and safe activities for your children to do.
- Keep a list of wholesome fun to do with your spouse and a list to do with girlfriends.

Prayer

Pray *The LORD guards you as you come and go, now and forever.* [PSALM 121:8 GW]

DAY 4

Focus on Guests

And he brought them into his house and set
food before them, and was overjoyed, since
he had become a believer in God together
with his whole household. Acts 16:34

Welcome Smiles

Juliette, aged six, opened the door with a huge smile and
a hug when I rang the bell. She asked me to come in and
sit. She explained that her mom would come when she finished what she was doing. She offered some cookies she
made and a drink.

The entire stay, Juliette showed wonderful hospitality
as did her family. When her pal came to play, she let her
pick out a game and take the first turn. She rejoiced when
her friend won and laughed with her friend when she won.

Juliette's heart of hospitality focuses on other people.
She came by it naturally from her parents who are so gra-
cious and love the Lord. When we model hospitality, our
children learn to serve others.

Read Acts 16:25-34. What made the jailer invite Paul and Silas to his home and what emotions did he show?

_____

_____

How did the jailor care for his visitors?

_____

_____

Read Acts 18:27-28. How did people show they cared about Apollos and wanted other people to welcome him when he travelled?

_____

_____

Read John 14:3 where Jesus talks about heaven. How will Jesus welcome believers?

_____

_____

_____

Read Acts 28:1-6. How did the native people treat Paul and the men who had been shipwrecked?

_____

_____

Read Acts 28:7-10. How did Paul respond to the hospitality?

_____

_____

What makes you feel welcomed and how do you welcome guests?

_____

_____

A Welcome Begins at the Door

- Have a friendly door sign or welcome mat.
- Smile before you open the door.
- Pass out hugs or words that express you are glad they have come.
- Introduce visitors to members of your family they haven't met.
- Show guests the bathroom, comfortable spots to sit, and the bedroom for overnight guests.
- Avoid rushing to finish cooking or chores. Let the answering machine take messages, etc.
- If guests stay for a meal, invite them to chat in the kitchen as you finish preparations.

Read Luke 10:38-42. Who welcomed Jesus into the house?

_____

_____

Contrast the actions of Mary and Martha.

_____

_____

Read 1 Peter 4:9. How does complaining make guests feel?

_____

_____

How did Jesus react when Martha complained? What did he point out was the better choice?

_____

_____

What meals can you prepare easily or before guests arrive, so you have time to enjoy them?

_____

_____

What distracts you when guests visit?

_____

_____

Read Matthew 8:14-15. How did Peter's mother-in-law react after being healed?

_____

_____

Read Genesis 43:33-34. Notice that Joseph observed a custom of the Egyptians. How do you react when someone from another culture visits?

_____

_____

_____

Develop a Guest-focused Attitude

- Greet your guest with enthusiasm and smiles.
- Have a comfortable and clutter-free area to sit with guests, whether it's in a living room, kitchen, patio, or other common room.
- Turn off the television and other distractions.
- Offer simple refreshments like a cold or hot drink and a snack that's ready to serve (fruit, cookies, crackers, chips).
- Look the person in the eye and listen.
- Ask questions about the person and their interests.
- Relax, laugh, and enjoy the time together. Be yourself and be polite.
- Express thanks for the visit and ask them to return.

Do your children feel you will welcome their friends for play dates?

_____

_____

How do you teach your children to welcome visitors?

_____

_____

Biblical Hospitality

Abraham, an old man, looked up and saw strangers approaching in the distance on a hot sunny day. He ran to them. He said that if he found favor with them, "please don't simply pass by." He offered to wash their feet and give them rest. He prepared a meal. These were activities of his many servants, but his attitude was that of a servant.

In Biblical times, people traveled by foot often and relied on strangers to help them. People who exercised hospitality did so with generosity. Abraham walked with his guests as they left to send them off. Today people drive away but we can send them off by standing and waving until they are out of sight.

Read Genesis 18:1-8. How did Abraham welcome the strangers?

_____

_____

Read Genesis 18:16. How did Abraham continue showing hospitality?

_____

_____

When have you entertained overnight guests? What experiences made it good?

_____

_____

Read Luke 9:1-6. What did Jesus' disciples bring and what did they trust would be provided?

_____

_____

When have your children had a friend sleep over and how did you help your children make that a good experience for the guest?

_____

_____

Be Prepared for Overnight Company

- Walk in your front door, look around and sniff the air. What's pleasant and what needs to be changed?
- Make sure the guest bathroom smells clean and has fresh towels and soap. Stock extra toilet paper, and empty the trashcan.
- Let children know if they can sit and chat, serve the snacks, or play with younger guests. If the time is for grownups share that they will need to play quietly or go to bed.
- Have fresh sheets on the bed.

- Prepare a spot for guests to use computers and easy access to plug them in for charging.
- Put out a basket with items guests may forget (toothbrush, toothpaste, comb, etc.).
- Keep some reading materials in the guest bedroom with a welcome note.
- Pray for guests before they arrive

Prayer

Read Hebrews 12:14. Pray for harmony and peace with guests

DAY 5

Home and Soul Fresheners

Unless the Lord builds the house, They labor in vain who build it; Unless the Lord guards the city, The watchman keeps awake in vain. PSALM 127:1

Bless Your Home

Scriptures remind us that God builds our real home, and He is the only one who can keep us safe. We may have storms and natural disasters, but they will not be a surprise to God.

Bless your home as a family to focus on the home being a blessing from God, to ask for God's protection and peace, and to ask him to guide you in using it for family and company.

Natural Disasters

I've lived from New England to Hawaii and Michigan to Florida. Everywhere there are different types of storms or problems that can impact homes. We've had severe damage from a category-four hurricane, plus damage from four lightning strikes, flooding, two spontaneous combustible fires, an earthquake, and even a derecho (sideways tornado). God kept us safe although we had lots of damage at times and none at other times. After repairs, we walked around the outside and inside praying for God to bless our restored home.

Read Matthew 5:45. On what people do blessings and disasters fall?

_____

_____

Read James 1:2-4. What attitude should you have concerning disasters?

_____

_____

Bible Home Blessing (2 Samuel 7:29, Luke 10:3-7)

David asked God to bless his home. He asked for God to bless it forever and for blessings upon the generations to come. He wanted God's peace and love to be in his home.

Centuries later Jesus sent His disciples out and told them to say, "Peace be to this house." when they entered a home. If a person of peace lived there, God's peace would rest on them. This shows us that we can pray a blessing on any home we enter (Luke 10:1-6).

Refreshed as Mothers

We need breaks and to be refreshed. Motherhood is hectic and demanding. It can be hard to get away, so find ways to relax at home. Unlike Jesus, we can't sneak out early and withdraw. We can draw our children in and close the doors for a little family retreat or quiet time without technology and outside noise.

Read Mark 1:35-36 and 7:24. What did Jesus try to do?

_____

_____

_____

Read Luke 5:16. What did Jesus do regularly?

_____

_____

Read Mark 11:28. What did Jesus say about rest and weariness?

_____

_____

Create a Spot for Rest and Refreshment

- Set up a spot away from television, computers, and other electronics, even if it is a corner of a room.
- Place pillows on a chair or floor to create a prayer or rest area.
- Add a table to hold a glass of water or a candle (use battery operated candles with young children).
- Hang a verse that contains a restful thought.
- If your children like quiet spots, help them create a corner tent.
- Have a prayer bag with a blanket, pillow, Bible, and quiet sign to grab and use.

Know what relaxes you. It might be soaking in a hot tub with candlelight and sweet scents after children fall asleep. Or it might be Christian music, curling up to read a good book or cuddling and talking with your spouse. What do you do to end the day or begin the next day?

_____

_____

Read John 16:33. What does Jesus want to give us?

_____

_____

Read Luke 12:13-15. To make a home a haven it helps to create a peaceful, loving atmosphere. Children can easily squabble and fight. What did Jesus say about greed? Does greed in your children make it hard for them to share and be content? If so, practice stating gratitude each morning for blessings to set their minds on being thankful.

Read Proverbs 18:1. What is a cause of fighting?

Feeling Loved

One granddaughter loves to sit on or beside me. She also likes to do things with me, like cooking, playing, and walking. Sometimes she pushes her little sister away because she wants me to herself. We chat about how there's room for both of them to be with me. She can be reluctant, but soon realizes it's fun to all play or work together. Learning to be giving and less selfish helps stop squabbles. It takes patience to help children get along and all feel loved.

Developing Sibling Love

- Avoid making comparisons. Instead, value each child's uniqueness.
- Express love daily to each child.
- Praise your children for sharing, being cooperative, for talents and efforts.

- Spend time with each child.
- Let children talk things out once they are old enough. Tell them you trust they can resolve the problem and walk away.
- Do your best to be fair, but remind your children to be thankful for what they receive.

Curtail Comparisons

One of our children complained, "_____ has more ice cream than me." I took a scoop from the complainer and dropped it into the other child's bowl and said, "You should be happy with what I gave you. I tried to be fair and divide it evenly, but I wouldn't want you to be a liar, so now it's true."

Another mom's child complained his sibling had more cereal in his bowl. She suggested they each count the pieces of cereal. They said that was ridiculous. She said she never counted the cereal pieces either but tried to be fair. A little logic with simple steps can stop comparisons and help children be thankful.

After Isn't Over

Michael had a friend over to play. They had a grand time while emptying the toy box and toy closet all over the family room carpet. About thirty minutes before I expected Ben's mom to arrive and take her son home I asked them to clean up. Michael said, "Mommy, we want to play more. I promise I'll clean it all up after Ben leaves." I agreed, thinking it was generous of my son to do all the work.

Two hours after Ben left, I went back to the family room to find everything still out. I asked Michael why he hadn't cleaned up the toys.

Michael looked up, with his blue eyes open wide, and said, "But Mom, after isn't over."

He got me on that one. I hadn't defined a time, and he was right— after wasn't over. I quickly said, "After just ended." He started cleaning up.

"After" is a word that implies there will be an ending, but parenting doesn't have an ending, as long as the parent and child live. We get past hurdles of newborns waking often, potty training, and more. However, new challenges come, and parenting continues. Life will continue to be a blessed mess with precious moments. Live each day fully and enjoy the time with your children at each stage and age. Lean on God for understanding and wisdom to mother your child and meet their needs.

"After isn't over" is true of God too. He chose you to be a mother and knows that with His power in you, you are good enough. He always loves us, forgives us, stays with us, rejoices over us, and guides us. When you feel you do not measure up, remember God's promises.

Psalm 121:5-7 _____

Psalm 137:7 _____

Isaiah 41:13 _____

1 John 1:9 _____

Zephaniah 3:17 _____

1 Thessalonians 5:5 _____

Philippians 4:13 _____

> *So do not worry or be anxious about*
> *tomorrow, for tomorrow will have worries*
> *and anxieties of its own. Sufficient for each*
> *day is its own trouble.* MATTHEW 6:34 AMP

Prayer

May the end of Joshua 24:15 be the prayer for your home: *as for me and my house, we will serve the Lord.*

CONTRIBUTORS

Linda Goldfarb is married to Sam, the momma of four adult children, "Maw- Maw" to many grandchildren. She is also an award-winning author of the LINKED Personality series, an international speaker, the founder of Parenting Awesome Kids, and a board-certified advanced level Christian life coach specializing in relationship management.

Speaker, author, coach, multi-interviewed **Yvonne Ortega** helps women who face challenges move from broken to beautiful, through her *Moving from Broken to Beautiful Book* Series, even when they feel overpowered. Yvonne celebrates life at the beach where she blows bubbles, builds sandcastles, and dances.

PeggySue Wells parasails, skydives, snorkels, scuba dives, and has taken (but not passed) pilot training. Solo mom of seven and founder of SingleMomCircle.com, she is the bestselling author of 30 books including The Ten Best Decisions a Single Mom Can Make, Homeless for the Holidays, and Chasing Sunrise.

To have Karen speak to your
group or organization,
contact her at authorkarenwhiting@gmail.com

WALKING HAND IN HAND AS CHRIST'S LOVE
transforms lives

MEETING THE
DEEPEST NEEDS

WE BELIEVE THE GOSPEL IS TRANSFORMATIVE
And you can change the world one child at a time.

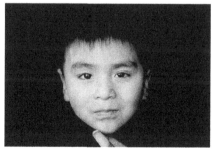

Thousands of children in the world are born into a cycle of poverty that has been around for generations, leaving them without hope for a safe and secure future. For a little more than $1 a day you can provide the tools a child needs to break the cycle in the name of Jesus.

OUR CONTACT

 423-894-6060

 info@amginternational.org

 @amgintl

 6815 Shallowford Rd. Chattanooga, TN 37421

Made in the USA
Middletown, DE
13 May 2022

65591138R00144